I AM THE WAY

Finding the Truth and the Life Through a Biblical Reimagining of the Tao

A NEW DEVOTIONAL
INCLUDING THE

Tao Te Ching

RH Martin, JD, MSW

Cover image © Shutterstock.com

www.kendallhunt.com
Send all inquiries to:
4050 Westmark Drive
Dubuque, IA 52004-1840

DEDICATION

To Dennis Geesey, who saw beyond the classroom's frame,
Where words took flight, and dreams found their aim,
In the fertile minds of youth, you sowed the seed,
A belief in words, in dreams, in what could be freed.

You told us tales of prose and verse,
Encouraged us to write, to rehearse,
With each pen stroke, you nurtured our art,
With your guidance, we found a new start.

You saw in me a spark of light,
A potential hidden from plain sight,
You said I could make the mundane sublime,
Turn alleys into boulevards, in my own time.

To teachers like you, who plant the seeds,
In the hearts and minds of eager, young breeds,
Your legacy blooms in each word we pen,
For you, Mr. Geesey, I dedicate this, then.

In your honor, we continue to write,
To turn alleys into avenues of light,
For you believed in us, now let it be known,
Your lessons and love in our hearts have grown.

CONTENTS

CHAPTERS

PREFACE

I Am The Way: Bridging Wisdom Across Traditions

Welcome, dear reader, to a journey of discovery and transformation. Holding this book in your hands, you embark on a quest that has taken me through the landscapes of faith, philosophy, and personal revelation. "I Am The Way" is not just a title—it's a promise, an invitation, and a testament to the interconnectedness of the human Spirit and the wisdom that has guided us through the ages.

The genesis of this work stems from a profound realization—a realization that the teachings of ancient Eastern wisdom traditions and the wisdom encapsulated in the Christian faith share more than a few parallels. I was driven by a question that echoed in my heart: What if we could synthesize the boundless love exemplified by Jesus with the profound life-enriching practices taught by Eastern Masters? This question became my compass, pointing me toward the crossroads of faith and philosophy, where "I Am The Way" took shape.

At its core, Christianity imparts the message of embracing the Love of Jesus as the path to enlightenment and salvation. Eastern Masters have long taught that cultivating Love, Compassion, and Wisdom opens the doors to discovering "The Way." It's a harmonious convergence of teachings, separated by time and geography, yet echoing the same resonant truth. "I Am The Way" seeks to unearth these ancient truths and weave them into a narrative that resonates with modern Christians seeking a deeper connection to their faith.

The Tao Te Ching, attributed to the sage Lao Tzu, is a revered text from ancient China that has illuminated the paths of wisdom seekers for centuries. The designation "Ching" refers to a classic book. Te is often translated as virtue, and Tao points to The Way. So, The Tao Te Ching is the Classic book of The Way of Virtue. Its teachings, centered on harmony, balance, and inner peace, have transcended time and cultural boundaries.

However, as profound as its insights are, its language and concepts will seem foreign to those rooted in Christian traditions. This is where "I Am The Way" comes into play—a bridge between two worlds, a linguistic and spiritual conduit that translates the Tao's wisdom into the familiar terms of Christianity.

I aim to foster a dialogue between Eastern philosophy and Western Christian thought throughout these pages. I draw parallels between the two, emphasizing the universal themes of love, grace, compassion, and the divine presence. By reimagining key concepts of the Tao Te Ching through the lens of Christian theology, I hope to offer readers a fresh perspective—one that encourages them to explore their relationship with God, humanity, and the world around them.

My journey in crafting "I Am The Way" was not only an academic exercise. I delved into the depths of my spirituality and embarked on a lifelong quest for understanding. From my experiences as a football player, prosecutor, defense attorney, social worker, therapist, mindfulness teacher, and happiness coach, the chapters of my life unfolded in unexpected ways, leading me from atheism to seeking, from Buddhism to Christianity, from the courtroom to the meditation mat, and from skepticism to unwavering faith. Each phase of my life contributed to the tapestry of wisdom woven into this book.

Life's twists and turns led me to delve into the teachings of Eastern masters, immersing myself in the wisdom of Taoism and Buddhism. The Tao Te Ching, a profound text, connected with my evolving spiritual journey during this phase. The Tao's elegant simplicity and insights into harmony, balance, and inner peace captivated me. I embarked on a transformative period of study and contemplation under the guidance of Taoist masters.

Meeting my wife was a turning point that led me to desire to create a "Rosetta Stone" that would enable us to discuss our cosmologies despite our differing backgrounds. My wife, a Southern Baptist Bible literalist, came from a different religious experience. Our union was a fusion of two contrasting cosmologies, each rich with its teachings and interpretations of life's purpose.

Early on, my wife's genuine sadness that I wouldn't be joining her in Heaven and my playful response about her not being reincarnated with me highlighted the intriguing crossroads where our beliefs converged and diverged. Our deep love for each other compelled me to explore how to bridge our spiritual worlds and facilitate meaningful discussions about our differing perspectives.

My wife's role as a sounding board, someone who could validate the effectiveness of my approach even from her conservative Christian perspective, was pivotal. Her positive responses to my interpretations of the Tao Te Ching and Christian teachings reaffirmed the book's potential to speak to a broad audience. As we discussed each chapter, I could see that bridging these two profound spiritual philosophies touched her deeply, demonstrating the universality of the book's message.

Throughout this journey, divine love guided me—the same love Jesus exemplified that permeates the teachings of the Eastern masters. This love, I believe, is the common thread that unites all seekers, regardless of their spiritual paths. It underlies our existence, inspiring us to fathom, empathize, and relate.

As you delve into these pages, you'll accompany me through my experiences of doubt and discovery, trauma and healing, love and loss. I hope you see echoes of your journey within these narratives, connecting with the universal threads of human experience that bind us all.

"I Am The Way: Finding the Truth and the Life Through a Biblical Reimagining of the Tao" is an endeavor to address the spiritual hunger that many feel in today's ever-changing world. It responds to the desire to connect with the Divine beyond strict doctrines, embracing the vastness of the human heart.

This book is not a manifesto but an exploration, an offering, and an opportunity.

You may wonder, why now? As the tides of change usher in a new era of interconnectedness through globalization, the internet, and interfaith dialogue, people seek novel ways to nourish their spiritual hunger. This book responds to that call, presenting a perspective that resonates with the openness of heart and mind that characterizes this evolving landscape.

Throughout this journey, I've encountered personal transformations and witnessed the impact of these teachings on others. Stories of connection, understanding, and healing emerged, confirming that the hunger for spiritual nourishment remains unabated. "I Am The Way" intends to strike a chord with those who seek, question, or explore spirituality, guiding them toward a more satisfying, meaningful, and serene existence.

So, I invite you to immerse yourself in these pages, explore the passages that resonate with your Spirit, and engage in the dialogue this book inspires. Together, let us walk the bridge that spans the wisdom of ancient traditions and the realities of our modern lives. Let us discover a new way, a harmonious convergence of East and West, of timeless wisdom and contemporary understanding. Welcome to "I Am The Way." The journey begins here.

In Unity and Love,

Bob Martin

In Gratitude to the Divine Unity

In humble reverence and deep gratitude, I acknowledge the divine presence that transcends all boundaries and manifests itself in the 10,000 forms. I offer my heartfelt thanks to the God of love and compassion, the source of grace and wisdom, whose light shines in the teachings of Jesus Christ. I also extend my appreciation to the Tao, the eternal Way, and the harmonious natural order it represents. I find guidance in its simplicity and wisdom.

I am indebted to the spiritual teachers and guides from Christian and Taoist traditions who have illuminated my path and shared their profound insights. Of special note are Master Hua Ching Ni, who first introduced me to the Tao, and, The Reverend Pastor Allen Cudahy of the Celebration Community Church and The Activation Church in Costa Rica, whom I love dearly, and who affirmed my understanding of Christianity.

My gratitude extends to the community of seekers who have joined us on this journey, offering their support, encouragement, and diverse perspectives. I celebrate the unity in the diversity of faiths and philosophies, knowing that we find common ground in our shared quest for wisdom and enlightenment.

May the wisdom of the Christ and the Tao guide us in every step of our lives, and may we continue to discover the profound interconnectedness of all things.

Of special mention and great thanks go to my Publisher, Angela Lampe, whose faith in me and this project brought it to the public. Her support and gentle guidance molded "I Am The Way" into a presentation I could not imagine. Heartfelt gratitude to my wife, Connie, who is a Bodhisattva, a Saint whose values and theology gave rise to the inspiration for this book. Thanks to The ECC Hombres, a small group of men I meet with every Monday morning, The Reverend Richard McBride, Ralph Waller, The Rev. Dr. Daniel H. Kuhn, Jr., The Rev. Dr. Jacob Luther Mauney, The Rev. Dr. Ray Pollard, Luigi Orlando, and The Reverend Bud Fisher, who bore my mood swings and steadfastly gave support, encouragement, wisdom, and most of all, kept me grounded. Thanks also to The Reverend Kirstin C. Boswell, Elon University's Chaplain, and the faculty and staff at The Numen Lumen Spiritual Center, who have inspired my interfaith journey.

My good friends, fellow curmudgeons, and Renaissance men, Albert Kauslick and Andres Benevente have been my mirrors, collaborators, buddies, and BFFs for as long as memory serves me. Albert, a magnificent artist created the image of Jesus and Lao Tzu joining paths. Andres, a designer of beautiful websites created the digital presence for the book and my life.

I want to thank and acknowledge Paul Mckenna, the Creator of The Golden Rule Poster, who graciously allowed the use of the poster. Paul has been spreading love throughout the world for years and we appreciate his good works.

Since joining the Elon Community Church, I have attended The Seekers Class, one of the Adult Sunday schools. It is a group where any question is allowed, and I have been free to express my Eastern thinking even as my understanding of Western theology has deepened. It has been the rails upon which my train of thought has traveled.

A gracious thank you also to Ning Marella, Mark Steven Rizarri, and Leah Mae Fernandez, who have tirelessly managed my social media and grown my platform so that my message can reach more eyes. Their assistance has taken a huge weight off my shoulders and allowed me the time to finish this project.

There are so many others: all my guest authors whom I asked for contributions, my Beta readers, friends, and family. They are too numerous to name them all, but I send my heartfelt thanks.

With a heart full of gratitude, I offer this devotional as a testament to the shared journey of Christians, Taoists, and all spiritual traditions. May it inspire and nourish the souls of all who read it.

ABOUT THE AUTHOR

RH "Bob" Martin

Bob's story is not a common one. He has had a diverse career and spiritual journey, including being a football player, prosecutor, social worker, therapist, and mindfulness teacher. He has also been a columnist and happiness coach, as well as exploring different religions such as Taoism, Buddhism, and Christianity. The anecdotes and experiences he has at his fingertips add color and excitement to the journey of this book.

The person who follows the way of Jesus or the Tao will live a practical, productive, meaningful, and contented life. Bob knows this to be true because this has been his journey. He is a 70+-year-old cheerful man. He enjoys close relationships with his second wife, his children, and her children.

He has had his share of trauma and battled his demons. Bob grew up selling cotton candy and hot dogs in amusement parks. His parents were Eastern European immigrants from Hungarian royalty on one side and Roma Gypsy on the other. The Bolsheviks slaughtered the royals, and, well, everybody slaughtered the Romas. So, his parents concluded that there could not be a God, and his family was atheist.

Even so, his father required him to attend children's Sunday School because "We are Americans, and you must know the Bible stories." Bob thought Old Testament stories were like fairy tales, but Jesus' unconditional love amazed him and he never forgot it. He was a chubby boy, bullied by boys and laughed at by girls. His parents were all business and not very affectionate. He never developed a sense of "hometown" as the family traveled so much. He could have gone under.

A profound belief that someone or something loves him somewhere out there strengthened him then and steels him now. That feeling of being loved leads him to know, as much as anyone can understand, that the universe's energy is good. Bob knows this because he feels it in those moments of stillness, in those rare moments when he forgets himself, in those thin moments when he feels connected to something much greater than himself.

He escaped the bullying of his junior years by becoming a football player and then a hippie after a career-ending injury. Then there was law school, a Juris Doctor, a prosecutor under Janet Reno during the cocaine cowboy days in Miami, and a mob lawyer.

His life went south in his 30s—a difficult marriage, and he was caught up in the glass and glitter of 1980s Miami partying.

One day, he went to see his therapist, George Robinson, about a profound crossroads in his life. He had started a business, which, in his arrogance, he believed would make him a millionaire. He was pouring money into it and came to a point where he would have to take a massive loan to make it to the finish line. He asked his therapist what he should do. George reached for a small cloth bag on the credenza behind him and extracted three Chinese coins.

George started shaking and throwing the coins on his desk, making numerical calculations, and drawing lines on paper. Bob looked on in disbelief. After all, Bob paid him $65 an hour, and George answered his urgent inquiry with hocus-pocus. Finally, George wrote a number, pulled open a book, turned to that number chapter, and showed it to Bob. The chapter title was one word—"Retreat."

Bob swore at him, stomped out, then drove around Miami seething, but knew he had to "retreat." Bob closed the business, did not take the loan, and earned his ability to work himself back from the brink. A few weeks later, Bob sheepishly returned to George's office and asked about the book. He told Bob it was the I Ching, The Classic Book of Changes. Then, Bob discovered George was the English language editor and disciple of Master Ni, Hua-Ching (née Hua-Ching Ni), a 72nd-generation Taoist master from the Shaolin Temple. Bob studied under Master Ni and George for eight years and engaged in contemplative practices. It changed his life.

In the late 80s, a conflict with his powerful clients led Bob to move to North Carolina, where he established himself in the community as an Assistant District Attorney and later opened a private practice.

His work with Taoism and Buddhism led him to close his law practice in 2000. He returned to school, earned a master's in social work, and became certified as a facilitator/teacher in two schools of meditation. He devoted himself to holistically representing indigent clients until his retirement. Then Elon University asked him aboard, where he continues to teach. This year, he became the Mindfulness Employee Resource Group coordinator. Shortly, he expects to teach meditation on campus as part of Elon's Wellness Programming.

Ever since he began questioning the nature of the universe at 15, Bob has loved Jesus as a wisdom teacher. He remarried to a Southern Baptist Bible literalist. Although it might seem odd, she is a Bodhisattva, a Saint. They connected on shared values of kindness and service.

Early on, she would be off to church on a Sunday morning and say goodbye with sadness in her eyes.

"What's wrong?" he would ask.

It's just that I love you so much, and I am sad that you won't go to heaven with me," she would lament.

"And I am sad that you won't be reincarnated with me," he would kid with a wink.

"Oh, stop that," she would say and be off.

They found a spiritual home at the open and affirming Elon Community Church (United Church of Christ), which is traditional enough for her and progressive enough for him. Today, she is happy that he, having been saved, will go to heaven with her, and he is glad she will be reincarnated with him.

DEAR READERS

I am thrilled to introduce my book, "I Am The Way," a humble attempt to explore the intersections between Biblical and Taoist philosophies. The book admits that merging the thinking of these two traditions has limitations because of their differences. However, it also highlights the significant similarities in values that make the endeavor worthwhile.

Christianity focuses on a personal connection with a relational God and the soul's salvation through faith in Jesus. Taoism, rooted in ancient Chinese wisdom, emphasizes living in harmony with the Tao, often translated as "The Way." This philosophy encourages simplicity, humility, and interconnectedness with the natural order. Although Christianity and Taoism differ, they share common ground on questions of virtue, conduct, humility, life, love, morality, and spirituality.

To help you navigate these differences and limitations, I have included an appendix in the book. In this section, you will find a standard translation of the 81 chapters of the Tao Te Ching. In respect of The Tao, I use the capitalized term, The Way, interchangeably with The Way of the Lord or The Way of God. I ask you to remember that reimagining text written in a nondeistic tradition into text compatible with a deistic practice can be challenging.

Comparing the chapters of the Tao Te Ching with their counterparts in "I Am The Way" will reveal similarities and significant differences. It is helpful to compare the two renditions, even though no one translation will provide a direct likeness. Writing this book involved extensive research and the synthesis of wisdom from various translations and texts. I consulted more than 15 translations, academic analyses, and popular commentaries on the Tao Te Ching. I then researched the Bible for similar themes, discussed them with advisors, and used my training and experience to formulate a path that honors both traditions while staying true to their essence, cadence, and style.

Essentially, "I Am The Way" explores the common ground between Christianity and Taoism, allowing you to take the best and leave the rest. It respects the love for Jesus Christ while breaking free from exclusivity and critical belief systems. It also honors the Tao by making its wisdom accessible to a broader audience.

I encourage readers to approach this book with an open heart and an open mind.

Embrace what resonates with you, find what is valuable and helpful, and grant grace for the rest. Although these traditions may differ, they share a deep concern for virtue, compassion, and the betterment of the human Spirit.

Thank you for embarking on this journey of spiritual exploration with me.

May you find inspiration, insight, and wisdom within these pages.

With gratitude and warm regards,

Bob Martin

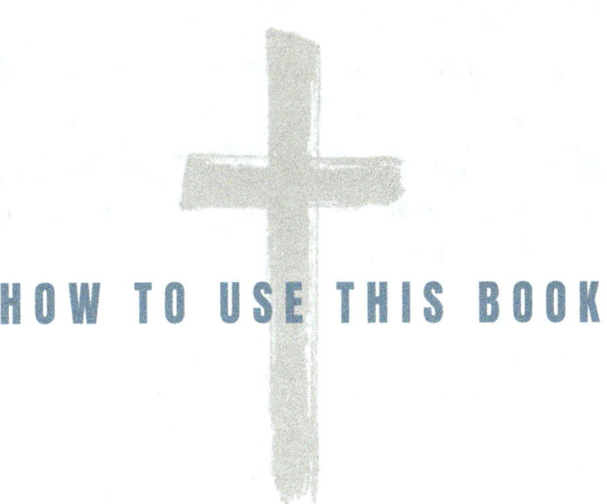

HOW TO USE THIS BOOK

This book is a journey of discovery, bridging the profound teachings of the Tao Te Ching with the wisdom of Christian traditions. If you want to enjoy and understand these insights, use this guide to help you read each chapter.

1. The book's structure follows the Tao Te Ching, with 81 chapters. Each chapter interprets the Tao Te Ching with a Christian perspective.

2. Read at Your Own Pace: "I Am The Way" is not a book to be rushed through. Its content is rich and thought-provoking, best enjoyed when savored and reflected upon. You can read a chapter a day, take it in over a week, or trust your intuition to guide you to the chapters that resonate with you.

3. Devotional or Discussion: Read the chapters in order or randomly, embracing the book as a devotional that offers daily inspiration. Use it to spark insightful conversations about the intersections of faith, wisdom, and spirituality in a group setting.

4. Dive Deep: Each chapter follows a structured format:
    *   Title: Sets the theme of the chapter.
    *   Famous Quote: Highlights a key theme from the text.
    *   Christian Interpretation: Presents a fresh Christian perspective on the Taoist wisdom, connecting the two traditions.
    *   Commentary: Expands on the interpretation, delving into the deeper meanings and implications of the text.

- Next Step: Offers a practical tip or action to integrate the teachings into your daily life.

5. Reflect and Apply: Reflect on each chapter's teachings. Consider how the interpretation resonates with your own beliefs and experiences. Think about applying the insights and practical tips to enhance your spiritual journey.

6. Comparisons and Appendices: In the appendix, you'll find a standard English translation of the Tao Te Ching for comparison. This can give you a broader understanding of the original text's nuances and inspire your reflections. It also may appear inconsistent with the text. I used more than 20 different translations to synthesize the themes of the Tao. I would encourage you to seek out additional translations.

7. Discussion and Sharing: Engage with others reading the book. Share your thoughts, insights, and questions. Sharing chapters with book clubs, friends, or online communities can expand your perspective.

8. Embrace Open-Mindedness: Approach each chapter with an open heart and an open mind. "I Am The Way" is a bridge between traditions, inviting you to explore the common threads that connect all paths to wisdom and spiritual growth.

9. Embody the Teachings: Remember that the true essence of this book lies in embodying the teachings in your life. While reading, consider how you can practice love, compassion, and wisdom in your daily interactions.

10. Savor the journey: Ultimately, savor the journey. "I Am The Way" is not about reaching an endpoint but about embracing the ongoing process of growth and understanding. Let the words guide, challenge, and inspire you to live a life of greater purpose, harmony, and fulfillment.

Whether seeking spiritual insights, exploring the intersections of faith, or simply curious about the wisdom these pages hold, "I Am The Way" invites you to embark on a transformative journey. May each chapter illuminate your path and lead you to deeper connections with your inner self and the world around you.

THE LEGEND OF LAO TZU AND THE WISDOM OF THE TAO TE CHING

In the heart of ancient China, amid the tapestry of history and myth, emerges a figure shrouded in mystery and wisdom—Lao Tzu. Born around 600 B.C., his name means "Old Master," a fitting title for a man who would leave an indelible mark on the world through his teachings captured in the "Tao Te Ching."

Lao Tzu's life is veiled in the mists of time, and some consider him a legend rather than a concrete historical figure. Yet, his legacy endures, a testament to the depth of his insights into the nature of existence and the human condition.

As the legend goes, Lao Tzu, disheartened by the turbulence of the world, embarked on a journey. He aimed to find solace in a quiet sanctuary where he could reflect on the mysteries of life. As he left his home, a city guard recognized his wisdom and pleaded with him to leave behind his teachings for posterity.

Heeding the guard's request, Lao Tzu penned down his thoughts, offering guidance for those seeking a harmonious way of living. The central pillar of his philosophy was the "Tao," often translated as "The Way." The Tao embodies the Universe's natural order, the essence that underlies all existence. It's the serene flow of rivers, the growth of trees, the ebb and flow of life—a harmony that invites us to align with the rhythms of the cosmos.

Within the pages of the "Tao Te Ching," Lao Tzu unveiled a treasury of profound insights. He advocated for humility, kindness, and compassion. He encouraged simplicity, urging people to find contentment in the present moment rather than chasing endless desires. His teachings resonated with Wu Wei, the idea of "effortless action," where one aligns with the natural course of events instead of resisting or forcing.

Lao Tzu's wisdom extended to understanding duality—the interplay of opposites. He posited that light and darkness, strength and weakness, are interconnected facets of the same reality. One can attain balance and harmony by embracing both sides, transcending the limitations of mere judgments.

One particularly captivating teaching is that true power is found in yielding rather than asserting control. In a world that often glorifies domination, Lao Tzu advocated for strength in vulnerability, for it's in yielding that we find our true essence and forge connections with the world around us.

As he concluded his writings, Lao Tzu handed the small yet profound book, the "Tao Te Ching," to the guard and disappeared into the mountains, leaving a legacy that would endure through millennia.

The "Tao Te Ching" remains a beacon of wisdom, its ripples felt across the ages. Its teachings have inspired countless seekers, philosophers, and thinkers throughout history. Lao Tzu's insights have transcended borders and cultures, resonating with the universal longing for understanding and harmony.

The legend of Lao Tzu and the "Tao Te Ching" resonates with us today, a poignant reminder of the enduring pursuit of balance, wisdom, and peace. It urges us to approach life with humility and kindness, embrace our strengths and weaknesses, and flow with the currents of existence rather than resist them.

Just as Lao Tzu ventured into the unknown, guided by inner wisdom, we too can navigate the complexities of life by drawing upon the teachings of the "Tao Te Ching." For in its pages lies a profound truth—that within the mysteries of existence exist a path to enlightenment and harmony that weaves through the tapestry of time and beckons us to find our own way.

CHAPTERS

In the beginning, there was emptiness.
Emptiness then creation.
Thus, the mystery from which all wonder arises.

CHAPTER 1

The Wonder and Mystery of God

"The most beautiful experience we can have,
is the mysterious."
Albert Einstein

The God that can be described
Is not the true God.
The Name that can be spoken
Is not the Name of God.
God is unnamable; the origin.
Naming God is the beginning of religion.
Let go, and you find God.
Holding on, you see the creation.
The Unnamable and the creation
Are ultimately the same.
Their source cannot be known.
All that can be known
Is that "I Am" is.
In the beginning, there was emptiness.
Emptiness then creation.
Thus, the mystery
From which all wonders arise.

COMMENTARY

The first teaching explores God's profound nature and how challenging it is to explain it in human language. It highlights that any attempt to comprehend God through words or names falls short of the true essence of the divine. Instead, the chapter suggests God is beyond any name or description.

In Exodus 3:14, God tells Moses His name is "I Am Who I Am" to show that He is eternal and unchanging, which is beyond our understanding. Isaiah 55:8-9 states that God's thoughts and ways are higher than ours, transcending our limited understanding.

"In the beginning was emptiness" echoes the concept of creation ex nihilo, where God creates the Universe out of nothing. This notion is present in Genesis 1:1: "In the beginning, God created the heavens and the earth."

The chapter proposes that the unnamable God and creation are the same, showing a deep connection between the divine and the created world. This echoes the biblical understanding of God's immanence, present in Colossians 1:17, "He is before all things, and in him, all things hold together."

This chapter asks you to consider God's mysterious nature, knowing humans can't entirely understand or describe it. Emphasizing the connection between the divine and creation encourages a respectful understanding of sacred mysteries. This chapter highlights the importance of the name "I Am" and how everything comes from the divine origin. It inspires amazement and curiosity about the sacred mysteries.

NEXT STEP

Embrace the mystery and wonder of existence. Rather than seeking to understand everything, learn to appreciate the beauty of the unknown and the vastness of the Universe. On a moonless night, leave the city lights behind and spend time with the Milky Way.

CHAPTER 2

Christ Transcends Opposites

> "The greater the contrast, the greater the potential.
> Great energy only comes from a correspondingly great tension of opposites."
> Carl Jung

If you view some things as beautiful,
You will view other things as ugly.
If you judge some people as good,
You will judge others as bad.
Opposites create each other.
There is no easy without difficult,
No long without short,
No high without low,
No before without after.
But Christ transcends opposites.
He acts without acting
And teaches beyond his words.
He does not resist what is,
Thus, His influence becomes irresistible.
He owns nothing yet has all.
He acts without regard to what people think.
He is Lord yet sees others as equal.
He fashions miracles and shirks pride.

He places importance only on the message.
When His work is done,
He moves on.
That is why his works are eternal.

COMMENTARY

Explore the concept of opposites and contrasts, emphasizing the dual nature of life and the limitations of human judgments. When we label things as beautiful or ugly, good or bad, we create an interdependent relationship between opposites. Additionally, in the realm of duality, there cannot be one aspect without the other—easy without difficult, long without short, high without low, and before without after.

The concept of opposites creating each other resonates with the biblical principle of balance and God's sovereignty. Ecclesiastes 7:14 says, "When times are good, be happy; but when times are bad, consider this: God has made the one as well as the other."

However, the chapter goes on to highlight how Christ transcends these opposites. It portrays Jesus as a divine figure who operates beyond human limitations, acting without striving and teaching beyond mere words. He doesn't resist what is but embraces and transforms it with an irresistible influence.

He embodied humility and selflessness, teaching through action, as seen in John 13:15 when He washed His disciples' feet. Jesus never resisted what was part of God's plan, humbly accepting the cross (Matthew 26:39).

Christ's ownership of all things is reflected in Colossians 1:16-17, declaring that all things were created through Him and for Him. Despite this authority, He treated everyone with equal love and compassion, breaking societal norms (John 4:9, Luke 7:39).

Jesus' focus on the message rather than worldly opinions is evident in Matthew 22:21, where He instructs to give to Caesar what is Caesar's and to God what is God's. He did not perform miracles for self-glorification but to reveal God's power and love (John 9:3).

Finally, the chapter highlights the eternal nature of Christ's works. When His mission is accomplished in one place, He continues His transformative work elsewhere, leaving a lasting impact and legacy.

This passage highlights the transformative power of Christ's teachings and actions, inviting us to shift our perspectives from judgment and dualism to embrace the eternal message of love, humility, and compassion.

NEXT STEP

Cultivate Nonjudgmental Awareness: Be mindful of your judgments and biases toward people, situations, and things. Practice viewing things from a perspective of nonjudgmental awareness, recognizing that opposites coexist and one's judgment may be limited or influenced by personal biases.

CHAPTER 3

Christ Leads by Showing The Way

"The best way to find yourself,
is to lose yourself in the service of others."
Mahatma Gandhi

The Lord did not promote himself,
And so empowered the people.
The Lord chose a donkey,
So that the people would not treasure stallions.
Christ leads by showing The Way.
He empties his mind of worldly desires.
He maintains honesty of Spirit.
He feeds the hearts of the hungry.
He strengthens faith.
He lets go of greed and avarice.
So that by contrast,
The cunning become known.
Acting with profound simplicity,
He allows the Father to flow through.

Appreciate the essence of Christ's selfless and humble nature and how it contrasts with the ways of the world. The Bible is replete with examples of how Jesus demonstrated these virtues.

The phrase "The Lord did not promote himself, and so empowered the people" reflects God's character. Throughout the Bible, we see God's focus on empowering His people, guiding them through challenges, and lifting them rather than seeking self-promotion (Exodus 13:21, Psalm 23:1-3).

The reference to the Lord choosing a donkey instead of a stallion (Zechariah 9:9) emphasizes the humility of Christ's triumphal entry into Jerusalem. It showcases how Jesus, as the King of Kings, chose a simple mode of transportation to illustrate His humility and approachability.

The chapter shows that Christ leads by offering The Way (John 14:6), emphasizing His role as the path to salvation and eternal life. Jesus emptied His mind of worldly desires, exemplified by His rejection of Satan's temptations in the desert (Matthew 4:1-11).

Christ maintained honesty of Spirit, teaching the truth and demonstrating integrity (John 18:37, John 8:31-32). He fed the hearts of the hungry physically, through miraculous feedings (Matthew 14:13-21), and spiritually, offering the living water (John 4:10-14).

Furthermore, Jesus strengthened faith through His teachings, miracles, and resurrection (John 20:29, Mark 9:24). He let go of greed and avarice, eschewing worldly riches (Matthew 19:21-24), teaching His followers not to store up treasures on Earth (Matthew 6:19-21).

The chapter suggests that the cunning are exposed through Christ's profound simplicity and humility. Jesus denounced the hypocrisy of religious leaders (Matthew 23:1-36) and warned against false prophets (Matthew 7:15).
Ultimately, Jesus allowed the Father to flow through Him, displaying perfect unity with God (John 10:30). He taught that anyone who had seen Him had seen the Father (John 14:9), emphasizing His divine nature.

This chapter captures the humility, selflessness, and profound wisdom of Jesus Christ. It inspires us to follow His example, letting go of worldly desires and allowing God to work through us to empower and uplift others.

NEXT STEP

Volunteer, Serve Others: Follow Christ's example of serving and empowering people. Seek opportunities to help and uplift others in your community and beyond. Serve with a genuine desire to make a positive impact, not for personal gain (Mark 10:45).

Nach-Noth/Shutterstock.com

CHAPTER 4

The Holy Spirit Is Never Used Up

> "The Holy Spirit is the bridge
> that connects our humanity to the divine."
> Archbishop Desmond Tutu

The Holy Spirit
Is like an ancient village well,
Inexhaustible, always putting forth.
When used, it is never used up.
It is mystery
From which all possibility arises.
It softens hard edges;
Loosens that which constricts;
Shades the unprotected;
And restores the damaged.
Paul knew this
When he asked us
To become one with the dust.
The dust from which we arose.
The origin of origins,
Beyond all-knowing.

COMMENTARY

Here poetic language and metaphors are used to convey the profound nature of the Holy Spirit's work in our lives. The imagery of an ancient village well, inexhaustible and continually putting forth water when used, represents the boundless and life-giving nature of the Holy Spirit (John 7:37-39).

The chapter portrays the Holy Spirit as a mystery, the source of all possibility (1 Corinthians 2:9-10). Through the Holy Spirit, God reveals His truths and profound spiritual insights to those who seek Him with a humble heart.

The Holy Spirit's transformative power is likened to softening hard edges and loosening that which constricts. This aligns with biblical teachings on the Spirit's role in transforming hearts and minds, making believers more receptive to God's guidance and love (Ezekiel 36:26, Romans 8:5-6).

The Holy Spirit also protects, shading the unprotected and restoring the damaged. In the Bible, the Spirit is often associated with being a comforter and advocate for believers in times of need (John 14:16, 2 Corinthians 1:3-4).

The reference to Paul asking us to become one with the dust from which we arose alludes to humility and a recognition of our origins and dependence on God (Genesis 2:7). Embracing our humble beginnings, we acknowledge God as the Creator and Sustainer of all things.

This teaching captures the mysterious and transformative nature of the Holy Spirit. It highlights the Spirit's role in providing spiritual nourishment, protection, and restoration. Just as a village well sustains and revitalizes a community, the Holy Spirit continuously works in our lives, guiding and empowering us as we seek to live in alignment with God's will.

NEXT STEP

Embrace Mystery and Faith: Recognize that the Holy Spirit is a mystery beyond complete human comprehension. Embrace the element of faith, trusting in the Spirit's guidance even when you may not fully understand its ways (1 Corinthians 2:9-10).

CHAPTER 5

God Is Loving and Just

> "Judge not, that you be not judged."
> Jesus Christ (Matthew 7:1)

God is loving and just.
His creation is impartial.
The sun rises on both
The evil and the good.
The Son of Man
Loves the righteous and unrighteous.
Thus, Godly ones
Adjust their behavior
In accord with the flow of Heaven.
Leaving judging to the Father
And following The Way of the Son.
Live from this center.

COMMENTARY

We can see God's love, impartiality, and desire for His followers to walk in His ways by living with love, compassion, and nonjudgmental attitudes toward others. By relying on God's guidance and the example of Jesus Christ, we are encouraged to align our behavior with the flow of God's will and leave judgment to Him. Living from the center of God's love and following The Way of the Son leads to a life of righteousness and compassion, reflecting God's character in our actions and relationships.

The chapter also reflects on God's loving and just nature and how His creation operates impartially, extending blessings to all. The reference to the sun rising on both the evil and the good emphasizes God's equitable treatment of all people (Matthew 5:45).

The phrase "The Son of Man loves the righteous and unrighteous" points to the unconditional love and grace of Jesus Christ, who came to call sinners and offer salvation to all (Matthew 9:13). This aspect of God's character encourages us to show compassion and love to both those who are righteous and those who are lost.

The chapter highlights that Godly individuals seek to align their behavior with the flow of Heaven, following God's will and purposes (Romans 12:2). They refrain from judging others, recognizing that ultimately judgment belongs to God alone (Matthew 7:1-2).

We are encouraged to follow the example of Jesus Christ, who is The Way, the Truth, and the Life (John 14:6). By living from the center of God's love and allowing His guidance to shape our actions, we reflect the character of Christ in our daily lives.

This chapter emphasizes the essential aspects of God's character—His loving and just nature—and how we are called to imitate Christ's love and compassion toward all. By adjusting our behavior in accordance with God's will and refraining from judgment, we can live harmoniously with God's creation and reflect God's love to others.

NEXT STEP

Research and Practice the Loving-Kindness Meditation, also known as the Metta Meditation. This ancient practice is designed to teach how to open the heart up to our loved ones and those we find challenging to deal with.

CHAPTER 6

God Gives Guidance and Support

> "Good and evil both increase at compound interest.
> That is why the little decisions you and I make every day
> are of such infinite importance."
> C. S. Lewis

God created
The male and the female;
Limits and the unlimited;
The conditional and the unconditional;
The creative and the destructive;
Guidance and Support.
They balance within God.
They exist within each of us.
We can use them any way we want.
They are always present.

COMMENTARY

This teaching acknowledges the multifaceted nature of God's creation and attributes. It high-lights God's creativity in forming both male and female (Genesis 1:27) and His omnipotence, where He sets both limits and the unlimited (Job 26:14, Psalm 147:5). It recognizes God's love and the existence of both the conditional and the unconditional aspects of His nature (John 3:16, Deuteronomy 7:9).

Creativity and destruction can coexist and God controls both (Isaiah 45:7, Psalm 104:30). It emphasizes God's role as a guiding presence (Psalm 32:8) and a source of support (Psalm 55:22) in our lives.

The chapter further points out that these attributes balance within God (Isaiah 40:12), illustrating His perfect harmony and wisdom. It also recognizes the indwelling of God's Spirit within each individual (1 Corinthians 3:16, 1 John 4:12), reminding us of our divine connection.

Lastly, the chapter acknowledges the free will given to humans to use these attributes in various ways (Deuteronomy 30:19). It reminds us of our responsibility to seek God's guidance and make choices aligned with His will (Proverbs 3:5-6).

This verse portrays a holistic view of God's creation and attributes. It encourages us to recognize the diversity and harmony of God's nature while inviting us to align our choices with His guidance. Acknowledging these aspects within ourselves reminds us of our inherent connection to the Creator and our responsibility to use His gifts wisely.

NEXT STEP

Self-Exploration: Spend time getting to know yourself better. Explore your strengths and weaknesses, the creative and destructive tendencies within you, the conditional and unconditional love you can express, and so on. Explore personality paradigms like the Briggs-Meyer and Enneagram personality inventories.

CHAPTER 7

God and Jesus Are Eternal

"Letting go gives us freedom, which is the only condition for happiness.
If, in our heart, we still cling to anything
—anger, anxiety, or possessions—we cannot be free."
Thich Nhat Hanh

Why is God eternal?
God was never born,
Thus, God can never die.
Why is God infinite?
God has no desire for self-praise,
Thus, God is present for all beings.
Why is Jesus eternal?
Jesus did not cherish His life
Above the lives of all creatures.
Because He has let go of Himself,
He is perfectly fulfilled.
Focusing on grasping this life
Imperils it.
Understanding this,
Suffering vanishes.

These verses emphasize the eternal nature of God, highlighting that God was never born and, therefore, can never die. They also explain God's infinite presence, as He has no desire for self-praise and is accessible to all beings. The chapter further addresses why Jesus is eternal, citing His selflessness and willingness to let go of His life for the sake of others. By prioritizing the lives of all creatures above His own, Jesus finds perfect fulfillment.

Psalm 90:2 describes God as everlasting from the beginning to the end. Psalm 139:7-10 speaks of God's omnipresence, being present everywhere and with everyone. Jesus' self-lessness is reflected in Philippians 2:5-8, where Jesus humbles Himself, takes on human likeness, and becomes obedient even to death. Galatians 2:20 further highlights the idea of "letting go of oneself," as Jesus calls us to live by faith in Him.

The overall message of the chapter urges us to embrace God's eternal and selfless nature, following the example of Jesus. We can find true fulfillment and overcome suffering by de-taching ourselves from selfish desires and serving others with love and humility. This insight aligns with the teachings of the Bible, encouraging us to focus on the eternal values of self-lessness, compassion, and service to experience a deeper connection with God and a more meaningful life.

NEXT STEP

Practice the Common Humanity Meditation: It is a practice designed to elicit feelings of connection and empathy. You can find a script or audio to listen to here: https://ggia.berke-ley.edu/practice/common_humanity_meditation

CHAPTER 8

God Nourishes All Things

> f you put water into a cup, it becomes the cup.
> You put water into a bottle, and it becomes the bottle.
> You put it in a teapot, and it becomes the teapot.
> Be water, my friend."
> Bruce Lee

God's love is like water,
It nourishes all things without trying to.
It is content to remain in the unseen.
The Lord's love is like water.
It is content with the low places
that people disdain.
Water gives life.
Immersion in water gives new life.
It shatters the shell surrounding the heart.
Therefore, be like the water of the Lord's love.
In dwelling, strengthen the foundation.
In thinking, keep to the task.
In conflict, offer abundance.
In leading, don't try to control.
In work, do what nurtures yourself and others.

In prayer, be completely present.
When you are content to simply be yourself
And do not compare or compete,
Everyone will respect you.

COMMENTARY

There are parallels between God's love and the qualities of water, emphasizing its nurturing, life-giving, and humble nature. Water's ability to nourish all things without striving aligns with God's boundless and unconditional love. As water remains unseen, God's love may not always be apparent, yet it is always present in our lives.

Luke 5 tells the story of Jesus calling His first disciples, including fishermen like Simon Peter. Water is a significant element in this narrative, symbolizing livelihood and cleansing. It highlights how God's love reaches even those in lowly places, just as Jesus called ordinary fishermen to become His followers.

The chapter also mentions that immersion in water gives new life, which resonates with the concept of baptism. Baptism represents a symbolic cleansing and rebirth, signifying the transformative power of God's love on the human heart. Jeremiah 4:4 and Psalm 51 both refer to cleansing the heart from impurities, akin to water breaking through the barriers around the heart.

The subsequent advice to be like the water of the Lord's love provides practical guidance on living a fulfilling and spiritually enriching life. Strengthening the foundation in dwelling alludes to building one's life on a solid spiritual footing. Staying focused on thinking and offering abundance in conflicts promotes a harmonious and generous approach to life. The call not to control in leading suggests a humble and servant-hearted leadership style akin to Jesus' teachings. In work, the emphasis on nurturing oneself and others reflects the principle of love in action.

Being present in prayer and finding contentment in oneself, free from comparison or competition, aligns with the biblical teachings of living in gratitude, humility, and self-acceptance.

This chapter poetically connects God's love with water's life-giving and transformative qualities, urging individuals to embody these virtues in their daily lives, rooted in biblical principles.

NEXT STEP

Practice being intentional about your intention. A good example is the saying of grace before meals. Extend this practice to other events. Develop a short blessing to silently utter when engaging in a task, such as, "I am writing this report for my benefit, the benefit of my coworkers and all creatures," or whatever works for you.

CHAPTER 9

A Full Mind Does Not Allow the Lord In

"True humility is not thinking less of yourself;
it is thinking of yourself less."
C. S. Lewis

A bowl filled to the brim
Does not allow anything in.
A mind filled with being right
Does not allow the Lord in.
Fame, gold, silver, admiration
Invite pride and arrogance
Then, disaster and the fall.
When His work was accomplished
The Lord withdrew and ascended.
When our work is accomplished
We are to surrender the glory.
This is the path to Heaven.

COMMENTARY

The teaching emphasizes the importance of humility, surrender, and avoiding arrogance. It draws parallels between a bowl filled to the brim and a mind filled with the need to be right, highlighting how being consumed by pride and self-righteousness prevents us from being receptive to the presence of the Lord.

Proverbs 16:18 warns against pride, as it leads to destruction. The call to surrender the glory and give credit to God resonates with passages like 1 Corinthians 10:31, which encourages doing all things for the glory of God. The chapter also reminds us of Jesus' humility in accomplishing His work and ascending to Heaven, as seen in Philippians 2:5-8 and Acts 1:9-11.

Overall, the chapter serves as a reminder of the path to Heaven, which involves emptying ourselves of pride, arrogance, and the need to be right. Instead, we are encouraged to be humble, receptive to the Lord's presence, and willing to surrender our accomplishments and glory to God. By adopting these attitudes, we can align ourselves with biblical principles and draw closer to the path of spiritual growth and connection with the divine. It underscores the significance of seeking a relationship with God through humility, selflessness, and acknowledging His work in our lives.

NEXT STEP

Research, Learn, and Practice Active Listening: Active Listening makes us aware of all our rehearsing thoughts that interfere with receptivity. Develop the habit of active listening in your interactions with others. Be open to different perspectives and be willing to learn from others' experiences and insights.

CHAPTER 10

Living in Harmony with the Sustenance of the Spirit

"The true meaning of life is to plant trees
under whose shade you do not expect to sit."
Nelson Henderson

Trees planted by streams of water
Sprout and grow in accord with the nourishment of Almighty gifts.
Prospering, they return gifts with great grace.
We are trees planted by streams of Spirit.
Can you live in accord with the nourishment offered?
Can you respect your soul, as well as its temple?
Can you be supple in mind and body
Like a child filled with awe and wonder?
Can you cleanse your heart of jealousy and avarice?
Can you lead with love and kindness born of inner wisdom,
Leaving Force, compulsion, and manipulation
In the valley where dead bodies and ashes are thrown?
Can you set your compass to mercy and compassion?
Can you deal with the most essential matters,
By influencing them the least?
Giving birth and nourishing without owning;
Treating all acts as vital and important,
Yet being unattached to the results.

Can you be engaged as if the Totum Factum,
Even while knowing to be only a cog.
Can you achieve without arrogance?
These are the instructions of the Lord.

COMMENTARY

This verse beautifully uses the metaphor of trees planted by streams of water to convey profound spiritual insights. The imagery depicts the flourishing of those who receive divine nourishment and grace. The reference to Psalm 1:3 emphasizes the blessed state of those who delight in God's law, much like trees rooted near life-giving water.

Drawing from Jeremiah 31:40, the verse encourages introspection and the pursuit of a virtuous life. It calls for cleansing the heart of negative emotions like jealousy and avarice, promoting love and kindness that stems from inner wisdom. The text highlights the significance of leading with mercy, compassion, and humility, echoing Micah 6:8.

The verse also emphasizes nonattachment to outcomes, as seen in Colossians 3:23-24 and Galatians 6:9. It encourages engaging fully in actions while surrendering the desire to control results, trusting in divine providence.

The instruction to deal with essential matters by influencing them the least aligns with the concept of yielding to God's will and recognizing that our role is merely a part of a grand design. This echoes the teachings of Proverbs 3:7-8, calling for humility and fear of the Lord.

Ultimately, the verse reflects a call to embody the divine qualities of love, compassion, and wisdom. By being receptive to the nourishment of the Spirit, cleansing the heart, and surrendering the ego, one can lead a life aligned with the instructions of the Lord. It encourages a deeper connection with the divine source, creating a purposeful and fulfilling existence.

Research and take a "drala walk." It's a practice of walking mindfully in nature while opening yourself to the inherent sacredness and energy present in the environment. The term "drala" roughly translates to "energy beyond aggression," emphasizing perceiving the world beyond our usual filters of concepts and judgments.

Eric M. Williams/Shutterstock.com

CHAPTER 11

God Fills the Space Within

> "The space within becomes the reality of the building."
> Frank Lloyd Wright

We may make a wheel with 100 spokes,
It is the empty hub that receives the axle.
We may fashion clay into a pot,
It is the emptiness within that gives it purpose.
We hammer wood to create a house,
It is the space within that supports life.
God formed mud into his favored creation.
It was what was within that gave it character.
If you stuff the hub with grain,
Pack the pot with silver and gold,
Load the house with discord and dispute,
You will shut the door to the Lord.
It is by emptying ourselves
That we fulfill our creation.
The material is useful.
The immaterial has timeless value.

This meditation shares spiritual wisdom about emptiness and the nonmaterial parts of ourselves. It shows how the empty center of things, like a pot or a house, holds their real meaning and importance. The verse also highlights that we, as God's favored creation, gain our character from what lies within.

The message is based on biblical principles of surrender and humility, emphasizing the importance of spirituality. Jesus exemplified the importance of emptying oneself and being humble (Philippians 2:7, Mark 8:34). Proverbs 4:23 and Matthew 12:35 speak of guarding one's heart and acknowledging the significance of what lives within. Colossians 3:2 and 2 Corinthians 4:18 call us to focus on heavenly values rather than earthly things.

The verse warns against the pitfalls of material excess and discord, which can obstruct our connection with God (Revelation 3:20). It invites us to empty ourselves of selfish desires and attachments to fulfill our true purpose, as seen in the teachings of selflessness and spiritual alignment.

Ultimately, this verse highlights the value of the immaterial, the timeless aspects of our being, and the significance of emptying oneself to embrace a deeper spiritual connection with God. It encourages a balanced perspective on material possessions while emphasizing the eternal value of our inner state and spiritual alignment. Integrating these principles into our lives allows us to find a greater sense of purpose, peace, and fulfillment in our faith journey.

NEXT STEP

Simplify and Embrace Emptiness: Reflect on areas of your life where unnecessary possessions, distractions, or conflicts may burden you. Embrace simplicity and declutter your physical and mental spaces. Allow room for emptiness, recognizing that it can hold profound meaning and purpose.

CHAPTER 12

The Wise Work with Devotion The Way

> "We must put guards at the portals of our mind."
> Gautama Siddartha

Ten thousand colors blind the eye.
Ten thousand sounds deafen the ear.
Ten thousand flavors numb the taste.
Ten thousand thoughts distract the mind.
Ten thousand desires harden the heart.
Satisfaction comes not
At the portals to the mind,
But in the fulfillment of the soul.
Therefore, the wise
Work with devotion to The Way.
Satisfy the stomach over the eyes and tongue,
And get along happily with much or little

COMMENTARY

This teaching profoundly reflects on the human experience, illustrating how sensory overload and excessive desires can distract and harden the heart. It emphasizes that true satisfaction and fulfillment are found in nourishing the soul and seeking devotion to The Way rather than indulging in an abundance of material pursuits.

The idea of sensory overload resonates with biblical principles. In Mark 4:19, Jesus warns about the deceitfulness of wealth and the worries of life, which can choke the Word and make it unfruitful. Similarly, in Luke 21:34, Jesus advises against being weighed down with carousing, drunkenness, and the anxieties of life.

Finding satisfaction beyond material pleasures aligns with teachings on contentment and seeking fulfillment in God. In Philippians 4:11-13, Paul speaks of learning to be content in all circumstances, finding strength in Christ. Pursuing material desires is also addressed in 1 Timothy 6:6, highlighting that godliness with contentment is great gain.

The verse's emphasis on working with devotion to The Way echoes Colossians 3:23-24, where Paul encourages us to work heartily for the Lord and not for human masters. It also aligns with Jesus' teachings on seeking first the kingdom of God in Matthew 6:33, trusting that all other things will be added.

Overall, the verse encourages a shift in focus from external distractions to inner fulfillment and devotion to The Way. By satisfying the soul through a deeper connection with God and finding contentment in His presence, we can experience genuine happiness and peace, regardless of our circumstances.

It offers a reminder to prioritize the spiritual over the material and to live with wisdom and devotion to The Way, seeking true satisfaction that transcends the limitations of worldly desires.

NEXT STEP

Limit External Distractions: Recognize that pursuing material desires and sensory indulgence can lead to dissatisfaction. Limit exposure to excessive stimuli. Consider if window shopping and browsing through catalogs is helpful to a calm mind or whether they stir up unnecessary wanting.

CHAPTER 13

God Wants Us to Love Ourselves

> "Love yourself first, and everything else falls into line."
> Lucille Ball

God's work is a success.
There is pain, suffering, disaster, and tragedy.
Then, is God's work a failure?
How silly to impose our assessments.
Reaching the zenith, the next move is down.
Lying at the nadir, the next move is up.
Both Job and Solomon would attest to this.
How silly to impose our assessments.
Aspiring to great success
And fearing failure
Present the same danger.
Better to accept our creation
Precisely as it is.
Learning to care for yourself,
You can care for the world.
Learning to love yourself,
You can love your neighbor
As yourself.

This verse reflects the human tendency to assess God's work based on our limited understanding, especially in the face of pain, suffering, and tragedy. It reminds us of the folly of imposing our assessments on God's divine plan, as His ways are higher than ours (Isaiah 55:8-9). The verse encourages us to recognize the cyclical nature of life, where ups and downs are part of the journey. Job and Solomon experienced the fluctuations of life, attesting to the ever-changing nature of circumstances (Job 1:13-22; Ecclesiastes 3:1-8).

The verse cautions against focusing solely on worldly success or fearing failure, as both can be dangerous distractions. Instead, it calls for acceptance of ourselves and our unique creation, trusting that God's plan for each individual is purposeful (Jeremiah 29:11). By learning to care for ourselves, we develop the capacity to care for others, echoing Jesus' command to love our neighbors as ourselves (Mark 12:31).

In summary, the verse urges us to humbly accept God's work and plan, embracing life's cycles with faith and trust. It encourages us to focus on inner growth, self-care, and self-love, recognizing that our capacity to love and care for others is rooted in how we treat ourselves. By aligning our hearts with God's wisdom, we can find peace and meaning amid life's challenges and joys.

NEXT STEP

Accept Life's Cycles: Understand that life has its ups and downs. Embrace the cyclical nature of experiences and recognize that success and failure are part of the journey. Make the phrase "This too, shall pass" part of your mental repertoire.

CHAPTER 14

Accepting the Mystery of God Brings Understanding

"The mystery of life isn't a problem to solve,
but a reality to experience."
Frank Herbert

Look for God.
There is nothing to be seen.
Listen for God.
There is nothing to be heard.
Reach for God; there is nothing to be held.
Invisible, inaudible, formless
Yet present, pervasive, and perceptible.
Holding all wisdom beyond wisdom,
All knowledge beyond knowing,
Subtle, beyond all conception.
In ancient days
Formless became form.
The invisible, visible. The inaudible, audible.
Live today by following in The Way.
And there will be new life.
Accepting the mystery brings understanding.

This contemplative verse reflects on the transcendent nature of God, emphasizing that while He may be unseen, unheard, and formless, His presence is pervasive and perceptible to those who seek Him with a humble heart. It acknowledges that God holds wisdom and knowledge beyond human comprehension and surpasses all conceptions. Drawing on the idea that the formless became form in ancient days, the verse highlights the mysterious ways God manifests Himself to humanity.

The text calls for living according to God's Way, following His teachings and commandments, which leads to a transformed life and a deeper understanding of His mysteries. By embracing the mystery of God's ways, we can find profound insight and wisdom beyond what human senses can perceive.

Psalm 46:10 encourages us to be still and know that God is present; Colossians 1:15, where Christ is described as the image of the invisible God, and 1 Corinthians 2:9 remind us that the depths of God's wisdom are beyond human comprehension.

Overall, this verse prompts us to seek God with faith and trust, recognizing that while His ways may be mysterious and beyond complete understanding, His presence and wisdom can be perceived in profound and transformative ways by those who earnestly seek Him.

NEXT STEP

Practice Silence and Stillness: Set aside time each day for quiet reflection and meditation. Embrace silence. Allow yourself to be still. For many, it isn't easy to be consistent with this practice. It is best to select a particular time. The morning works best for many. Try connecting it to another consistent routine, like having coffee.

CHAPTER 15

Let Your Faith Give You Patience

"The greatest test of faith is when you don't get what you want but still,
you are able to say: Thank you, Lord."
John Hagee

The wisdom of the Lord is profound and subtle.
Unfathomable, there is no way to comprehend it;
Only the teaching can be described.
The Lord taught us;
When your stomach is empty
Take the opportunity to fill your soul.
When the waters around you
Are muddy with sorrow, loss, and agony
Let your faith give you patience.
The mud will settle, and the water become clear.
When the powerful slap, mock, and curse you,
Relish in your lowly position and love God.
The tide of the Almighty will raise you up.
Be careful and alert when times are uncertain;
Courteous as a guest; generous as a host.
Do not be arrogant in new neighborhoods.
Those who practice these ways
Do not know tomorrow.

Not knowing, seeking, or expecting,
They are present and can welcome all things.

COMMENTARY

This pensive meditation reflects on the profound and unfathomable wisdom of the Lord, acknowledging that human understanding can only scratch the surface of His infinite knowledge. The poem draws upon teachings from Luke 6, where the Lord provides guidance for navigating life's challenges.

In times of emptiness and sorrow, the Lord's teaching encourages us to seek spiritual nourishment and solace in God's presence. As muddy waters eventually settle, our faith can bring clarity and patience to endure hardships.

When faced with insults and mistreatment, the Lord's instruction is to respond with humility and love for God, trusting that the Almighty will ultimately uplift those who endure with faith.

Uncertain times call for vigilance and a humble attitude. The verse emphasizes the importance of being courteous and generous, recognizing that we do not have complete control over tomorrow. Instead of seeking to predict or control the future, the verse suggests embracing the present with an open heart, welcoming whatever comes our way.

Overall, the verse highlights the wisdom of embracing the mystery of God's ways and living in the present moment with faith and humility. It echoes the teachings on seeking God's guidance, finding strength in adversity, and walking humbly with the Lord (Micah 6:8). It also echoes Jesus' teachings on responding to mistreatment with love and praying for those who persecute us (Matthew 5:44). By acknowledging the profundity of God's wisdom and aligning our lives with His teachings, we can experience a deeper understanding of our purpose and relationship with Him.

Research and Learn about the I Ching. This centuries-old practice of self-examination is designed to make us more sensitive to the times surrounding us. Although some think of the I Ching as an oracle, it is a method of cultivating patience and appropriate behavior.

andreev-studio.ru/Shutterstock.com

CHAPTER 16

You Can Deal with Whatever Life Brings You

"The quieter you become, the more you can hear."
Ram Dass

Blessed are those whose thoughts are few;
Whose hearts are at peace?
They can bear witness to suffering,
Yet maintain their stillness.
How can they do this?
Relying on treasured thoughts,
Brings confusion and discord.
Serenity and stillness call to the Holy Spirit.
Connected to the source,
You instinctively become tolerant, impartial, and amused;
As kindhearted as a grandmother;
As dignified as a King;
As productive as a loyal servant;
As Full of wonder as a child.
Immersed in the Spirit,
You can deal with whatever life brings you.
When death comes, you will be ready.

This chapter portrays the state of blessedness for those who possess a calm and peaceful heart, even amidst suffering. It emphasizes the power of stillness and serenity, which comes from relying on the guidance of the Holy Spirit. The verse suggests simplicity and a few essential thoughts are better than being confused and conflicted with too many thoughts.

Biblical references supporting these concepts include the teachings of Jesus in the Sermon on the Mount (Matthew 5:3-12). The Beatitudes speak of the blessedness of the meek, those who hunger and thirst for righteousness, and those who are peacemakers. These qualities align with having few and treasured thoughts, as well as maintaining inner peace amidst trials.

The text also touches on the fruit of the Holy Spirit (Galatians 5:22-23), which includes love, peace, and self-control. When connected to the source of divine wisdom and love, we naturally embody virtues like tolerance, impartiality, and kindness. This connection also fosters childlike wonder and awe for the beauty of life.

Being immersed in the Spirit aligns with the Apostle Paul's exhortation to be filled with the Holy Spirit (Ephesians 5:18), which empowers us to face life's challenges with readiness and resilience. Furthermore, the assurance of being ready for death resonates with the Apostle Paul's confidence in victory over death through Christ (1 Corinthians 15:54-57).

This meditation encapsulates the blessings from a heart at peace, relying on the Holy Spirit for guidance and embracing a simple, contented mindset. By cultivating stillness, serenity, and a connection to the source of divine love, one can face life's difficulties with grace and find readiness for whatever lies ahead, including the inevitability of death.

NEXT STEP

Maintain Inner Stillness: In moments of chaos or conflict, practice inner stillness and serenity. This is, of course, easier said than done. We generally try to quiet our thoughts by attempting to suppress them. However, what you resist persists. Instead, allow your thoughts to run free and give them all the attention they desire. Shortly, they will leave you be.

CHAPTER 17

Jesus Led as a Servant

"The greatest leader is not necessarily the one who does the greatest things.
He is the one that gets the people to do the greatest things."
Ronald Reagan

The leadership of God is so subtle,
The people must rely on faith.
Therefore, it transcends all contention.
Jesus led as a servant,
And so was loved and praised.
Rome led through lawful oppression,
Therefore, it was feared but understood.
The Pharisees led by pretending
To be of and for the people,
And thus were despised.
If the leaders do not trust the people,
They are not worthy of the people's trust.
Godly leaders, loving the people as family,
Speak honestly and do what they say they will do.
Trusting the people,
They empower.
So, the people grow in confidence and accomplishment.

COMMENTARY

The Bible speaks about the qualities of a good leader and the importance of leadership based on faith, love, and trust in God. In Luke 22:27, Jesus taught that authentic leadership is servant leadership: "For who is greater, the one who is at the table or the one who serves? Is it not the one who is at the table? But I am among you as one who serves."

1 Peter 5:2-3 also teaches that leaders in the church should not lord their authority over others, but rather should lead by example and with humility: "Be shepherds of God's flock that is under your care, watching over them—not because you must, but because you are willing, as God wants you to be; not pursuing dishonest gain, but eager to serve; not lording it over those entrusted to you, but being examples to the flock."

The idea of trusting the people and empowering them to grow in confidence and accomplishment is also reflected in the Bible. Proverbs 11:14 emphasizes the wisdom of seeking counsel from others: "For lack of guidance a nation falls, but victory is won through many advisers."

NEXT STEP

Read a biography of a leader who modeled the principles suggested by this text. Trust the people you lead and empower them to make a positive impact. Delegate responsibilities and provide opportunities for growth and development, fostering confidence and accomplishment.

CHAPTER 18

God's Religion Is Simple but Not Easy

"If you have something to say that is not helpful but is truthful,
refrain from saying it. If it is helpful but not truthful, avoid it.
If it is helpful and truthful, choose the right time to say it."
H. H. Dalai Lama

God's religion is simple.
It can be described in two words:
Love and Kindness.
To arrive at this simplicity
Requires great wisdom and effort.
Failing this, morality and judgment arise.
Hypocrisy becomes commonplace.
Without love in the home,
The people preach family values.
Without kindness in the culture,
Nationalism arises
And cleverness and self-interest step forth.
Man builds gilded temples of stone and mortar.
God builds temples in the heart.

COMMENTARY

The essence of this chapter reflects a profound truth found in various biblical teachings. God's religion is indeed centered on love and kindness, as emphasized by Jesus when he summarized the commandments as loving God and loving one's neighbor (Matthew 22:37-39). The Bible repeatedly highlights the importance of love and compassion in our relationships with God and others (1 Corinthians 13:4-8, Galatians 5:22-23).

The verse also points out that embracing this simplicity of love and kindness requires wisdom and effort. We are encouraged to seek wisdom, and the book of Proverbs, in particular, speaks extensively about the value of wisdom and understanding (Proverbs 2:6, Proverbs 4:7).

On the contrary, when love and kindness are lacking, the verse warns that morality and judgment may arise, leading to hypocrisy and division. The Bible cautions against hypocrisy and teaches us to be humble in our opinions (Matthew 7:1-5, James 4:11-12).

Furthermore, the chapter highlights the consequences of neglecting love and kindness in various spheres of life. Without love in the home, the mere preaching of family values may ring hollow. In the absence of compassion in society, divisive tendencies like nationalism can emerge. The Bible instructs us to show love and kindness to others (1 Peter 4:8, Ephesians 4:32).

The verse highlights that God's true temple is not physical structures but the transformed heart. Paul affirms this concept, teaching that God dwells in the hearts of those who believe in Him (1 Corinthians 3:16, 1 Corinthians 6:19-20).

In summary, this verse encapsulates the fundamental teachings of God's religion found in the Bible, emphasizing the importance of love, kindness, wisdom, and the transformation of the heart as the essence of a faithful life.

NEXT STEP

Set an Intention to Be Mindful of Your Words: Watch your speech carefully, ensuring your words are kind, truthful, and uplifting. Avoid gossip, judgment, and divisive language. When you notice your speech falls below your standards, correct it and quickly make amends. You are your best teacher.

CHAPTER 19

Place Greater Value on the Simple and Effective

"Simplicity is the ultimate sophistication."
Leonardo da Vinci

Those that hoard piety,
Invite empty ritual and judgment.
They would never heal on the Sabbath.
Those who hoard wisdom and intelligence,
Invite exclusivity and argument.
They may lose contact with the ground.
Those who hoard knowledge and facts,
Invite cleverness and confusion.
They become lawyers and clients of their own making.
Those who hoard silver and gold,
Invite robbers and thieves.
They surrender all security and peace.
These things have their place,
But they are not sufficient.
Look at all the suffering
Caused by the myriad of ancient laws.
It is better to place greater value
On the simple and effective.

Love your God with all your heart, soul, and mind
Love your neighbor as yourself.

COMMENTARY

This chapter highlights the pitfalls of hoarding various aspects of life and the superiority of simplicity and love. It draws attention to the consequences of excessive accumulation and attachment to external possessions and knowledge. The verse echoes the teachings of Jesus, who often emphasized the significance of genuine love and inner transformation.

In Mark 2:27, Jesus challenges the religious leaders' rigid adherence to the Sabbath laws, emphasizing that the Sabbath was made for man, not man for the Sabbath. This demonstrates the importance of genuine piety and compassion over mere adherence to ritualistic practices. The verse suggests that focusing solely on religious rituals and judgment can lead to spiritual stagnation and a lack of healing and growth.

The verse also warns against hoarding wisdom and intelligence, which can lead to pride, exclusivity, and contentious arguments. The notion of losing contact with the ground indicates a detachment from reality and a potential disconnect from humble human experiences.

Hoarding knowledge and facts can foster cleverness and confusion, leading to a fixation on legalistic interpretations and self-made systems. Similarly, accumulating silver and gold can attract thieves and robbers, symbolizing the loss of security and peace.

The verse emphasizes that while these things have their place, they are insufficient for a meaningful and fulfilling life. The ultimate value lies in simplicity and effectiveness, as Jesus taught, loving God with all one's heart, soul, and mind and loving one's neighbor as oneself (Matthew 22:37-39). This reflects the essence of Christian teachings, emphasizing the transformative power of love and compassion, which surpasses all material and intellectual accumulations.

NEXT STEP

Reflecting on Ancient Laws: Consider the impact of strict adherence to ancient laws or dogmas. Evaluate whether they contribute to spiritual growth and well-being or create unnecessary suffering.

CHAPTER 20

Do Not Hasten for the Lavishness of Feasts

"Let no one ever come to you without leaving better and happier.
Be the living expression of God's kindness:
kindness in your face, kindness in your eyes, kindness in your smile."
Mother Teresa

Do not hasten after
The wisdom of the wise;
The discernment of the discerning;
The power of the powerful;
The strength of the strong.
The people revel in the extravagance of feasts.
They are spellbound by the promise of holidays,
And treasure their myriad things.
There is such tenacity, desire, and surplus.
Should I not fear what they fear?
Covet what they covet?
Nonsense!
I follow The Way of the Lord.
He chose what is foolish in the world,
To shame the wise.
He chose what is weak in the world,
To shame the strong.

He chose what is low and despised in the world,
To reduce to nothing things that are popular and craved.
He is the source of my life.

COMMENTARY

This teaching emphasizes the futility of chasing after worldly pursuits and the wisdom of following The Way. The writer urges not to be enamored by the knowledge, power, and possessions valued by society. Instead, they find solace in following God's path, which may seem foolish or weak in the eyes of the world.

The passage aligns with the teachings of the Apostle Paul, who reminds us that God's wisdom often contradicts human wisdom. In 1 Corinthians 1:18-19, Paul highlights that the message of the cross may appear foolish to some, but it is the power of God to those who believe. God often chooses the weak and despised to confound the wise and strong, as stated in 1 Corinthians 1:27. The Christian perspective encourages a shift in focus from the material abundance and status sought after in the world to a life centered on faith, love, and humility.

Ultimately, the verse echoes the call to seek the Kingdom of God and His righteousness, as stated in Matthew 6:33. It reminds us that true wisdom, strength, and fulfillment come from aligning our lives with God's will and purpose. By following The Way, we find a source of energy that transcends worldly desires and provides a deeper meaning and understanding of existence.

NEXT STEP

Let Go of Fear: Release the fear of missing out (FOMO) or coveting what others have. Trust that there is a plan for your life, and have faith that another chapter is always coming.

bbernard/Shutterstock.com

CHAPTER 21

Great Virtue Cannot Be Held in the Hand

"The best and most beautiful things in the world
cannot be seen or even touched
they must be felt with the heart."
Helen Keller

Great virtue cannot be held in the hand,
Yet, it can be grasped.
Great virtue cannot be seen with the eyes,
Yet its manifestation can be observed.
God cannot be held in the hand,
Yet the essence of God can be grasped.
God cannot be seen with the eyes,
Yet the manifestation of God can be observed.
We have attempted to explain the force that is God
Yet, it has remained elusive;
Elusive, mysterious, subtle, indistinct.
Unquestionably genuine, it can be trusted.
From the beginning of time,
The force of God has imbued all things.
How do I know this?
It is infused within me.

COMMENTARY

This chapter reflects on the intangible nature of great virtue and God's essence. It highlights the paradox that while these profound qualities cannot be physically held or seen, their effects and manifestations are evident in our world. The text points to the idea that God's presence and influence can be observed through the wonders of creation and the workings of life.

Job 36:26 speaks of God's incomprehensible nature, while Isaiah 55:8-9 reminds us that God's ways are higher than ours. These verses echo the sentiment expressed in the text, acknowledging that God is elusive and beyond complete human understanding, yet the genuine impact of God's presence is unmistakable.

The verse also emphasizes the personal experience of God's presence, stating, "It is infused within me." This resonates with the biblical concept of God's Spirit dwelling within us (1 Corinthians 3:16), fostering a deep, spiritual connection with God.

The verse invites readers to acknowledge the mystery of God's nature while recognizing God's undeniable influence and presence in their lives and the world. It encourages embracing the profound virtues of love, kindness, and trust in God, even if the entire understanding of God remains elusive to human intellect.

NEXT STEP

Research and consider the practice of Lectio Divina. This practice is designed to cultivate the ability to allow yourself to spend enough time with a concept or scripture so that it sinks deeply within you and integrates with your Spirit.

Great virtue cannot be held in the hand, yet it can be
grasped. Great virtue cannot be seen with the eyes,
yet its manifestation can be observed.

CHAPTER 22

Whoever Loses His Life Will Find It

> "There is a crack in everything; that's how the light gets in."
> Leonard Cohen

To become whole,
First, flaws must be acknowledged.
To become straight,
First, crookedness must be accepted.
To become filled,
First, emptiness must be embraced.
To become rich,
First, little must be desired.
To have great strength,
First, weariness must be achieved.
To achieve new life,
First, death must be experienced.
To become confused,
First, covet all things.
If you want to be given all things,
First, surrender all things.
By residing in the grace of the Father,
Christ set an example for all beings.
By not claiming credit for himself,
His merit is treasured.

Because he seeks nothing from others,
The people can trust his words.
Because He is not self-righteous,
The people can enjoy humility.
Because He does not glorify himself,
The people bask in His glory.
Because He does not compete with the world,
The world can never overcome Him.
"Whoever wants to save their life will lose it,
but whoever loses their life will find it."
It is the only way to be made whole.

COMMENTARY

To become whole, the Bible teaches the importance of acknowledging one's flaws (1 John 1:8), accepting our crookedness (Proverbs 3:5-6), and embracing our emptiness, recognizing our need for God's filling (Ephesians 3:19).

True richness comes from desiring little and finding contentment in God's provision (Philippians 4:11-13). Great strength is achieved through weariness, relying on God's power in our weakness (2 Corinthians 12:9-10).

To experience new life, we must die to ourselves and be born again in Christ (John 3:3-5). Confusion results from coveting all things, but surrendering everything to God leads to His abundant blessings (Matthew 6:33).

Following Christ's example of humility, selflessness, and not competing with the world, we find true glory in God's grace (Philippians 2:3-8). Jesus teaches that to find life, we must lose it for His sake (Matthew 16:25). This selfless surrender is the only way to be made whole in Him.

NEXT STEP

Set aside time each day for self-reflection. Acknowledge your flaws and imperfections honestly without judgment. Embrace the crookedness and emptiness within you. Allow yourself to explore these aspects with compassion and a willingness to grow. Take a self-compassion break.

CHAPTER 23

Bearing Witness, the Path Is Found

"When the winds of change blow,
some people build walls, and others build windmills."
Chinese Proverb

A tornado will not last all morning.
Even nature cannot sustain a thunderstorm for long.
It is destructive, but nonetheless, the work of Heaven.
Anger will not last all morning.
Temptation is not sustained for long.
These are troubling, but nonetheless, the work of Heaven.
It is in bearing witness, not perfection, that the path is found.
Thus, one who seeks God embraces the universal truth.
One who seeks The Way embraces universal virtue.
One who seeks the Spirit embraces the universal essence.
One who seeks loss fails to find the path.
If you seek God, God eagerly accepts you.
If you seek the Lord, the Lord is happy to receive you.
If you seek the Spirit, the Spirit will fill your soul.
If you seek loss, loss will be delighted to have you.
Nevertheless, the door to Heaven is still open to you.
None of this is apparent.
It must be trusted, or there will be confusion.

This text carries spiritual and philosophical insights, drawing from both the natural world and theological concepts.

The opening lines remind us of the impermanence of natural phenomena. The reference to a tornado and a thunderstorm not lasting all morning echoes the Book of Ecclesiastes, where Solomon observes, "To everything, there is a season, and a time to every purpose under heaven" (Ecclesiastes 3:1). Just as nature's destructive forces are part of God's creation, they also have their appointed times.

The verse suggests that anger and temptation, though powerful, are not sustained indefinitely. The Bible advises against harboring anger for prolonged periods: "In your anger do not sin: Do not let the sun go down while you are still angry" (Ephesians 4:26).

The verse encourages us to embrace universal qualities when seeking God, the Lord, or the Spirit. This mirrors biblical principles of seeking righteousness and virtue. In the Gospel of Matthew, Jesus teaches, "Blessed are those who hunger and thirst for righteousness, for they will be filled" (Matthew 5:6).

The verse introduces the intriguing idea of seeking loss, suggesting an opportunity for spiritual growth even in our failures and defeats. This concept parallels the biblical notion that God is always ready to welcome repentant hearts, as seen in the parable of the prodigal son (Luke 15:11-32).

The concluding lines stress the importance of trust and faith in the spiritual journey. Hebrews 11:6 states, "And without faith, it is impossible to please God because anyone who comes to him must believe that he exists and that he rewards those who earnestly seek him."

In summary, this verse intertwines natural observations with spiritual insights, invoking biblical wisdom to emphasize the transient nature of life's challenges, the importance of seeking God and virtue, and the significance of trust in the divine journey. It encourages us to embrace the cycles of existence and find solace in the ever-open door to Heaven through faith and humility.

Cultivate the Tolerance of Discomfort: Notice when you experience moments of emptiness or vulnerability and embrace them rather than trying to fill them with distractions. Check in with yourself. Ask, "What thoughts am I having? What body sensations are present?" You can learn to tolerate and be more present by deconstructing your feelings.

Cammie Czuchnicki/Shutterstock.com

CHAPTER 24

Hold Fast to What Is Good

> "Love and compassion are necessities, not luxuries.
> Without them, humanity cannot survive."
> H. H. Dalai Lama

Those who strive to rise above others,
Will find themselves alone.
Those who claim to be wiser than they are,
Have lost the wisdom of Heaven.
Those who boast, praise, and flaunt themselves,
Stray from The Way of the Lord.
Did not even gilded Rome
In its self-proclaimed glory,
Fall like rubbish?
And Moses denied the promised land,
For his arrogance?
These things are worldly but not at all useful.
Therefore, bless those who have lost The Way.
Bless and do not curse them.
As cursing is nothing more
Than self-ingratiating babble.
Hold fast to what is good.

Love one another with mutual affection.
Do not be haughty.
Do not claim to be wiser than you are.
Live peaceably with all.
Be ardent in Spirit.
Serve the Lord.

COMMENTARY

This teaching offers wisdom on humility, righteousness, and the pitfalls of arrogance. It draws upon biblical and moral principles to convey a message of modesty, love, and service to the Lord.

The verse begins by cautioning against the ambition to rise above others, highlighting that such endeavors can lead to isolation. Jesus emphasized that "whoever exalts himself will be humbled, and whoever humbles himself will be exalted" (Matthew 23:12).

It warns against claiming to be wiser than one truly is, suggesting that such self-aggrandizement results in a loss of heavenly wisdom. The Apostle Paul wrote, "Do not deceive yourselves. If any of you think you are wise by the standards of this age, you should become 'fools' so that you may become wise" (1 Corinthians 3:18).

The verse underscores the perils of boasting and self-flattery, emphasizing that these behaviors divert one from the path of the Lord. This sentiment aligns with the biblical teaching that "Pride goes before destruction, a haughty spirit before a fall" (Proverbs 16:18).

The reference to Rome's downfall and Moses' denial of the promised land are cautionary tales against arrogance and worldly glory. In the Bible, Moses was denied entry to the Promised Land due to a moment of pride and disobedience (Numbers 20:12). Rome's decline serves as a historical reminder of the impermanence of worldly empires.

The verse urges a compassionate response to those who have lost their way, encouraging blessings and discouraging cursing. This aligns with Jesus' teachings in the Sermon on the Mount: "Bless those who curse you, pray for those who mistreat you" (Luke 6:28).

The verse closes with exhortations to hold fast to goodness, love one another, live peacefully, and serve the Lord with ardor. These principles resonate with various biblical passages, such as Romans 12:18, which advises, "If it is possible, as far as it depends on you, live at peace with everyone."

NEXT STEP

Seek True Wisdom: Instead of boasting about our knowledge or wisdom, pursue genuine understanding and seek wisdom from those around you that fills you with a sense of goodness and peace. Please make a list of those models and pay attention to their habits and values.

CHAPTER 25

Before Heaven and Earth Were Born

"We are all star-stuff, contemplating the stars."
Lawrence M. Krauss

Before Heaven and Earth were born,
Before the Universe
Was something complete in itself,
It may be regarded as the Creator of all things.
Bringing design and structure to the chaos.
So far beyond humankind's conception,
It cannot be called by a specific name,
It is the subtle essence of the Universe.
In the absence of an accurate word
And yearning to have some access,
We call it "God."
Grasping for more understanding,
We attempt descriptions:
Serene, Solitary, Unchanging, Infinite, Present
Ethereal, Changeless, Undisturbed, Ceaseless,
Impalpable and Everlasting,
Extending without limit.
Ultimately returning to its self-sufficient origin,
It shares its wisdom with all Nations.
Yet only the math and formulae of genius

May give any hint of its operation.
Humans follow the natural law of the Earth.
The Earth follows the natural law of the Universe.
The Universe follows the natural law of God.
God only follows its integral nature.

COMMENTARY

This chapter reflects on God's timeless and incomprehensible nature as the Creator of all things. It acknowledges that before the creation of the heavens and the Earth, something complete and divine existed beyond human understanding and description. The verse embraces the concept of a transcendent and omnipotent God who brings order and structure to the chaos of the Universe.

The reference to "God" in this context aligns with various biblical passages that speak of God's eternal nature, creative power, and wisdom. The Bible describes God as the ultimate source of all existence and the one who sustains the entire Universe.

For instance, Genesis 1:1 reveals that God is the Creator of the heavens and the Earth. Psalm 90:2 describes God as "from everlasting to everlasting," emphasizing His eternal existence. Romans 1:20 speaks of God's invisible attributes, lasting power, and divine nature evident through the creation.

The verse emphasizes God's awe-inspiring nature and human language's limitations to capture His essence fully. It acknowledges that while we attempt to grasp and describe God's attributes, our understanding will always fall short. Nevertheless, it encourages seeking wisdom from God, recognizing His integral nature, and following His natural laws that govern all creation. By humbly acknowledging God's sovereignty, we align ourselves with the divine order and purpose of our lives.

NEXT STEP

Nature Walks: Spend time in nature and observe the beauty and intricacy of creation. Connect with the natural world as a reflection of God's design and structure. Let the wonders of nature inspire a sense of humility and reverence.

CHAPTER 26

Don't Be Distracted by Golden Calves

"The secret of success is constancy of purpose."
Benjamin Disraeli

The root of the great Oak is heavy.
The branches and leaves are light.
It is the heavy that builds the foundation for the light.
The air in the house of mourning is heavy.
The air in the house of feasting is light.
The Godly understand
First, attend to the heavy,
To create space for the light.
When given a task, the Godly approach it
As a charge from the Lord,
And take it seriously.
They make full use of all resources,
And never let their attention
Be distracted by golden calves,
And other gorgeous things.
Once their task is complete
And their gear safely stored,
They can relax.
How can the lords of the fish, the fowl, the cattle,

And every creeping thing
Apply themselves lightly to the world?
To be light is to lose one's root.
Without a root, all that is left are
Infants, tossed back and forth by the waves,
And blown here and there by every wind.

COMMENTARY

This chapter illustrates the wisdom of the Godly in understanding the balance between the heavy and the light aspects of life. The analogy of the great Oak's heavy root, providing a solid foundation for the delicate branches and leaves, emphasizes the importance of attending to the foundational aspects of any task or endeavor. This concept aligns with biblical principles of seeking wisdom and strength from God to build a solid foundation.

The contrast between the heavy air in the house of mourning and the light atmosphere in the house of feasting reflects the natural ebb and flow of life's experiences. The Bible acknowledges joy and sorrow, encouraging us to find solace in God during mourning and to give thanks during feasting (Ecclesiastes 3:4; Philippians 4:6).

The Godly are portrayed as diligent and serious in their approach to tasks, seeing them as charges from the Lord. This aligns with biblical teachings on serving God with wholehearted devotion and using one's talents and resources to glorify Him (Colossians 3:23; 1 Peter 4:10).

The caution against distraction by worldly pursuits, symbolized by "golden calves" and "gorgeous things," resonates with biblical admonitions to avoid idolatry and materialism (Exodus 20:3; Matthew 6:19-21).

The verse's conclusion emphasizes the importance of staying rooted in God's ways to avoid being tossed around by worldly influences. This echoes biblical teachings about finding security and stability in God's Word and will (Psalm 1:3; Ephesians 4:14-15).

In summary, this verse offers insightful wisdom about prioritizing life's heavy (foundational) aspects, maintaining godly diligence, and remaining steadfast in God's truth to find stability and purpose.

Rest and Find Balance: After completing tasks and fulfilling your responsibilities, take time to rest and recharge. Store your physical and mental gear, and find moments of relaxation and tranquility to rejuvenate yourself.

Artorn Thongtukit/Shutterstock.com

CHAPTER 27

Being Skillful at Life

> "The mediocre teacher tells. The good teacher explains.
> The superior teacher demonstrates. The great teacher inspires."
> William Arthur Ward

If we are to follow in The Way,
We would travel the world
Without planting flags.
We would speak skillfully,
And keep no records of wrongs.
We would care for the least of these
As both vocation and avocation.
Polishing our craft as a helper,
We would hone our craft
As those of a Master Carpenter
Or an able seaman.
We would love everyone,
And reject no one.
We would care for all creation.
This is called salvation.
Thus, the skilled become the teacher of the unskilled.
And the unskilled become the teacher of the skilled.
The teacher who does not take the student to heart,
And the student who does not value the teaching,
Are both deluded and lost,

No matter how learned they may be.
This is profoundly important.

COMMENTARY

In this reflection, the chapter profoundly explains what it means to follow in The Way. They emphasize the importance of humility, compassion, and skillful living, drawing inspiration from various biblical principles.

The chapter echoes Jesus' teachings, who called His followers to walk in The Way, characterized by love, selflessness, and service to others. It reflects the teachings of caring for the least of these, as mentioned in Matthew 25:40, where Jesus identifies with the needy and the marginalized. The call to care for all creation resonates with the biblical message of stewardship, recognizing that God created everything and entrusted it to us.

Keeping no records of wrongs aligns with the biblical concept of forgiveness. Colossians 3:13 urges us to forgive others as the Lord forgave us. The importance of being skilled and humble, becoming both a teacher and a student, reflects the biblical principle of discipleship. In 2 Timothy 2:2, Paul encourages passing on knowledge and skills to others who can, in turn, teach more.

The overall theme of loving everyone and rejecting no one echoes the commandment to love our neighbors as ourselves, stated in Mark 12:31. The commentary beautifully captures the essence of salvation, as salvation is not merely a ticket to heaven but a transformative process of living out God's love and purpose on Earth.

This reflection serves as a reminder of the core teachings of Christianity, urging us to be genuine followers of The Way by exemplifying love, humility, and care for both humanity and creation. It emphasizes the significance of sincere discipleship, valuing learning from others, and teaching those seeking wisdom. Indeed, this reflection embodies the essential truths at the heart of the Christian faith.

NEXT STEP

Stewardship of Creation: Care for all creation by adopting sustainable practices, reducing waste, and showing respect and appreciation for the environment and the resources entrusted to us. Respectfully encourage others to do the same.

CHAPTER 28

Keeping a Strong Back and a Soft Heart

"The greatest enemy of knowledge is not ignorance,
it is the illusion of knowledge."
Daniel J. Boorstin

The Divine created the opposites;
The Masculine and the Feminine,
The Light and the Dark,
The Mountain and the Valley,
Honor and Disgrace,
To define, complement, and sustain each other.
The worldly see them in competition.
Can we shed our delusion?
Can we keep a strong back and a soft heart?
Can we stand in the light of acclaim,
And retire into the shadow of a humble abode?
Can we honor the truth of science,
While still basking in the mystery?
Those who traded their worldly comfort
For the higher understanding
Become models for the world.
Knowing the glorious and keeping to the lowly,
They become the valley of the world.

Lifting all things,
They abide in virtue and return to the state of uncarved wood.
Ready to be carved into instruments
Of the Lord

COMMENTARY

This reflective chapter beautifully explores the divine balance and harmony in creation, where opposites such as masculine and feminine, light and dark, mountain and valley, and honor and disgrace coexist to define, complement, and sustain each other. It challenges us to see beyond the worldly perspective that views these opposites in competition and invites us to embrace unity in diversity.

The passage echoes the biblical truth of God's creation, where from the very beginning, God created male and female in His image (Genesis 1:27). It reminds us that the existence of light and dark is part of God's design (Isaiah 45:7). It calls us to appreciate the beauty of both the exalted moments in the light of acclaim and the humble abode in the shadows.

It poses essential questions about shedding delusions, cultivating a strong back and a soft heart, and honoring the truth of science while embracing the mystery of God's creation. It encourages a balanced approach to knowledge and humility, where we seek understanding without losing sight of the awe-inspiring mysteries that only God comprehends fully.

The passage draws inspiration from Jesus' teachings about finding higher understanding by letting go of worldly comforts (Mark 8:35) and becoming models for the world through humble service (Matthew 23:11). It reflects the call to be the valley of the world, lifting others through selfless love and abiding in virtue.

Ultimately, the passage conveys the profound message of embracing the divine balance, being open to growth and transformation, and surrendering to God's creative process. Just as uncarved wood is ready to be shaped into instruments of the Lord's design, we are called to be vessels in His hands, allowing Him to carve out His purpose in our lives. This reflection challenges us to live with purpose, humility, and love, becoming instruments that resonate with God's divine melody in this intricate symphony of creation.

Embrace Both Sides: Acknowledge and embrace the opposites in life, whether masculine and feminine qualities, light and dark moments, or honor and disgrace. Understand that these opposites are part of the grand design and can work together for a greater purpose.

CHAPTER 29

The Gift of God

> "Think of the rivers of blood spilled by all those generals and emperors
> so that in glory and triumph, they could become the momentary masters
> of a fraction of a dot."
> Carl Sagan

In God's eye,
Our Earth is a tiny blue dot.
In His vast creation
It has been given to us,
Yet it is not ours.
Nothing can be added to it,
And nothing taken away.
We do not hold the creative force.
Although in our arrogance, we imagine it so.
This has always been our disgrace.
God put eternity in our hearts and made us mortal.
A cruel joke or a keyhole to our promise?
So, The wise align themselves with God's Earth
"For everything there is a season,
and a time for every purpose under heaven:
A time to be born and a time to die."
Therefore, we should eat and drink,

And enjoy good in all our labor.
This is the gift of God.

COMMENTARY

This insightful chapter contemplates the grandeur of God's creation and the insignificance of our Earth in comparison. It acknowledges that while the Earth has been given to us, it ultimately belongs to God, and we do not hold the creative force. The verse laments humanity's historical arrogance in claiming mastery over a mere fraction of this vast universe, recognizing it as our disgrace.

The passage references the bloodshed caused by human ambition, reflecting on the futility of pursuing temporary glory and power on this tiny blue dot in God's creation.

Yet, amid this perspective, the verse acknowledges that God has placed eternity in our hearts while making us mortal. It questions whether this is a cruel joke or a keyhole to our promise, hinting at the tension between our earthly limitations and our spiritual longing for something greater.

In light of this contemplation, the wise align themselves with God's purposes and timing, as described in Ecclesiastes 3:1. They recognize a season for everything under heaven, including a time to be born and a time to die.

The conclusion is one of embracing the gift of life that God has given us. We should enjoy the fruits of our labor, finding satisfaction in all we do, as it is a gift from God (Ecclesiastes 3:13).

This reflective verse offers a humbling perspective on our place in the universe, acknowledging our limitations and the importance of aligning ourselves with God's will and timing. It serves as a reminder to appreciate life's gift and find joy and purpose in our labor, all within the context of God's eternal design.

NEXT STEP

Practice Compassion and Justice: Reflect on the consequences of human arrogance and the suffering caused by ambition for temporary glory. Seek to live a life of compassion, love, and justice, making a positive impact in the lives of others.

CHAPTER 30

Sometimes, Tables Must Be Overturned

"In peace, sons bury their fathers.
In war, fathers bury their sons."
Herodotus

The Way of the Lord is peaceful
And does not oppress by force of arms.
Those who engage or counsel war
Do not follow in The Way.
They rely only on their own strength.
Thus, they are subject to those who are stronger.
For those who take up the sword,
Perish by the sword.
Those who oppress by force,
Do not follow The Way.
Thus, they are subject to the ten plagues.
Sometimes, tables must be overturned.
Then nations must hold dear,
And, above all, return to The Way.
They must seek an end to war for victory's sake.
Instead to engage only
To safeguard its people, not dominate,

To achieve the purpose and nothing more,
To achieve the purpose without arrogance,
To achieve the purpose and then extend a hand.
And pray, as Solomon, for wisdom.
War is unstable and disruptive.
The peace of God is eternal.
Forsaking the peace of God,
Leads to an early end.
This is true of each of us,
Not just nations.

COMMENTARY

This verse emphasizes the peaceful nature of The Way and condemns oppression through force and war. It draws upon biblical principles that promote peace, wisdom, and the avoidance of violence. Several Bible citations align with the themes presented:

The Way of the Lord is Peaceful:

Isaiah 2:4: "He shall judge between the nations and shall decide disputes for many peoples, and they shall beat their swords into plowshares, and their spears into pruning hooks; nation shall not lift sword against nation, neither shall they learn war anymore."

Matthew 5:9: "Blessed are the peacemakers, for they shall be called sons of God." Matthew 5:44: "But I say to you, Love your enemies and pray for those who persecute you." Philippians 4:13: "I can do everything through him who strengthens me." Proverbs 3:5-6: "Trust in the Lord with all your heart, and do not lean on your own understanding. In all your ways, acknowledge him, and he will direct your paths." James 1:5: "If any of you lacks wisdom, let him ask God, who gives generously to all without reproach, and it will be given him."

The verse reminds us that relying solely on human strength, seeking dominance, and engaging in violence leads to destruction and instability. Instead, it calls for nations and individuals to embrace the peace of God, pursue His purpose with humility, and extend a hand of compassion and understanding. Forsaking the peace of God is detrimental and can lead to an early end, both for nations and individuals.

This reflection urges us to be peacemakers and align ourselves with The Way, seeking wisdom through prayer and living out God's peaceful and purposeful plan. By embracing God's eternal peace and forsaking violence, we can experience the true blessings and fulfillment of walking in The Way.

NEXT STEP

Avoid Oppression: Refrain from oppressing or taking advantage of others through force or manipulation. Treat others with fairness, kindness, and respect, recognizing their inherent value as fellow creations of God. Cultivate the courage to speak out against any oppression you observe.

The good General does not wage war to take glory in victory or to avenge. For avenging is the province of the Lord. He mourns his fallen and those of his enemy and attends funerals of grotesque proportions.

CHAPTER 31

The Best Use of Hard Strength Is to Enable Soft Strength

> "The ultimate weakness of violence is that it is a descending spiral,
> begetting the very thing it seeks to destroy.
> Instead of diminishing evil, it multiplies it."
> Martin Luther King Jr.

God created the material from the chaos.
He created a time to be born,
And a time to die.
Thus, the destructive force,
Is inside the creative force.
Man created weapons and the military.
This is called perversion.
Some live to perfect them.
The good General seeks to avoid war.
The bad General delights in the slaughter of men,
And sees peace as the dull time between wars.
Thus, has wholly lost The Way.
The worldly way honors strength.
The Diplomat commands the soft strength.
The General commands the hard strength.
The Godly General knows,
His best use of hard strength is to enable the soft strength,

And to only use the hard strength
When there is no other choice
To prevent even more harm.
The good General does not wage war
To take glory in victory or to avenge.
For avenging is the province of the Lord.
He mourns his fallen and those of his enemy.
And attends to funerals of grotesque proportions.

COMMENTARY

The teaching provided reflects a profound insight into the duality of creation and destruction, the complexities of human nature, and the pursuit of peace in a world marred by conflict and violence. It echoes several biblical principles and themes found throughout the Scriptures.

The concept of creation from chaos is central to the Bible's opening verses in Genesis 1:1-2, where God brings order out of a formless void. Ecclesiastes 3:1-2 emphasizes the divinely appointed time for every event, including birth and death.

The passage speaks of the tension between the creative and destructive forces, which can be understood through Isaiah 45:7, where God declares His sovereignty over light and darkness, prosperity and calamity. The Bible doesn't explicitly address the creation of weapons and military in this context, but it does caution against misuse of power and violence (Matthew 26:52).

The contrast between the good and bad General is reminiscent of biblical teachings about seeking peace and avoiding war if possible (Romans 12:18). It reflects the importance of following The Way and honoring strength for righteous purposes (Proverbs 24:17-18).

The Godly General's understanding of using strength to enable peace aligns with biblical teachings on pursuing justice, mercy, and humble service (Micah 6:8).

The passage's mention of mourning for the fallen and the pursuit of peace is akin to the beatitude in Matthew 5:9, "Blessed are the peacemakers, for they shall be called sons of God."

The verse encompasses deep insights into human nature, the struggle between peace and conflict, and the call to seek godly wisdom and compassion.

NEXT STEP

Mourn and Honor the Fallen: In times of conflict and loss, grieve for those who suffer, regardless of their affiliation. Remember that every life is precious and deserving of respect. Attend funerals of those friends who have lost loved ones. This is the path to cultivate compassion and increase your tolerance of discomfort.

CHAPTER 32

The Law of Heaven Can Be Written on Our Hearts

"Science without religion is lame.
Religion without science is blind."
Albert Einstein

The Creative Force is beyond understanding.
We give it a name,
So we can pretend to explain and control it.
This is called religion.
We study it.
We name it the Unified Force Field or the Prime Mover.
This is called science.
Yet, no one in the world can manage or master it.
We can perceive its subtle essence.
This is called following The Way.
If kings and ministers would embrace it,
The Kingdom of Heaven would reign on Earth,
And the work of lawmakers would dwindle
As the Law of Heaven would be written on our hearts,
And sweet dew would fall.
There are already so many labels and regulations.
We must become as accomplished river pilots,

Gently guiding our canoes
Down the stream of righteousness and justice
Into the expansive sea
Of the unnamable and unknowable.

COMMENTARY

The chapter reflects on the ineffable nature of the Creative Force, often attributed to God, and the human attempts to understand and control it through religion and science. It draws parallels between different ways people seek to comprehend the mysteries of existence. The passage acknowledges the limitations of human knowledge and underscores the importance of humbly following The Way, which leads to righteousness and justice.

The idea of the Creative Force being beyond human understanding is supported in the Bible, particularly in passages like Romans 11:33, which speaks of God's unfathomable wisdom and knowledge. Additionally, Proverbs 30:4 acknowledges that human attempts to grasp the divine entirely are limited.

The passage critiques the tendency to name and regulate the Creative Force through religion and science. While the Bible encourages seeking knowledge and wisdom, it also warns against claiming complete mastery over divine mysteries (Job 11:7).

The concept of perceiving the subtle essence of the Creative Force resonates with the call to be still and know that God is. Psalm 46:10 emphasizes a contemplative approach to understanding God's presence.

The verse's call for kings and ministers to embrace The Way aligns with biblical teachings on seeking God's will and righteousness to establish the Kingdom of Heaven on Earth (Matthew 6:10).

The imagery of becoming accomplished river pilots, gently guiding canoes down the stream of righteousness and justice, mirrors the biblical idea of walking in the ways of the Lord (Proverbs 3:5-6) and letting God's law be written on our hearts (Jeremiah 31:33).

In conclusion, the verse provides a thought-provoking meditation on the limitations of human understanding and the importance of humility and righteousness in approaching the unnamable and unknowable Creative Force. It encourages embracing The Way and seeking the Kingdom of Heaven through righteous living and obedience to God's guidance.

NEXT STEP

Explore the awe-inspiring photos captured by the James Webb Space Telescope. As you examine the stunning images of distant galaxies, nebulae, and cosmic phenomena, take a moment to fathom the staggering scale of the universe. Contemplate the inconceivable distances and time spans involved, and let the sheer magnitude of these numbers inspire a sense of wonder and humility.

CHAPTER 33

Be Content with What You Have

> He who is not contented with what he has
> would not be contented with what he would like to have."
> Socrates

Those who place their attention on others
May become knowledgeable,
And tie themselves to Earthly concerns.
Those who place their attention on their souls
Develop their relationship with God,
And tap into the wisdom of the Lord.
Following The Way is not easy.
So, we distract ourselves by controlling others.
True strength is in having the discipline
To maintain Godly ways.
For those who want more,
Finding contentment is as difficult
As a camel passing through the eye of a needle.
Those who live in the Kingdom
Are content with what they have.
And are wealthy beyond measure.
Those who have found the Way
Are born into a new life,
And their grace will be remembered forever.

This teaching delves into the dualities of human focus and their spiritual consequences, drawing parallels with Biblical wisdom. Placing attention on others while potentially fostering knowledge may tether one to transient earthly concerns (Philippians 2:3-4). Conversely, directing attention to the soul promotes a deeper relationship with God, enabling access to divine wisdom (James 4:8).

The verse emphasizes the challenges of the spiritual journey ("Following The Way is not easy"), and it notes how, as a diversion, some might attempt to exert control over others (Matthew 7:13-14). However, the true strength lies in disciplined adherence to godly principles (1 Corinthians 9:25).

Contentment is portrayed as an arduous pursuit ("Finding happiness is as difficult as a camel passing through the eye of a needle"), echoing Christ's teachings on the challenges of detachment from worldly desires (Matthew 19:24).

The contrast between living in God's Kingdom and being content with what one possesses aligns with Paul's insights about being content in all circumstances (Philippians 4:11-12). Such contentment transcends material wealth, resonating with Christ's teachings on seeking God's Kingdom first (Matthew 6:33).

The verse highlights that those who embrace The Way of spiritual enlightenment experience profound transformation ("born into a new life"). This renewal echoes Christ's teachings on being born again (John 3:3), leading to an enduring legacy of grace (2 Corinthians 5:17).

In summary, this verse resonates with biblical teachings by addressing the tension between focusing on worldly matters and spiritual growth. It underscores the challenges of maintaining godly discipline and finding contentment amid life's complexities. Ultimately, the verse highlights the transformative power of embracing the spiritual Way, leading to renewed vigor and lasting grace.

NEXT STEP

Let Go of the Desire for Control: Release the need to explain and control the Creative Force through human constructs like religion or science. Instead, embrace a posture of surrender and trust. Consider adopting the phrase, "I don't know. That's above my pay grade."

CHAPTER 34

The Spirit Is Like the Wind

"The wind that gave our grandfather his first breath
also received his last sigh.
The wind also gives our children the Spirit of life."
Chief Seattle

Only God's Spirit gives new life.
The Spirit is like the wind that blows wherever it wants to.
You can hear the wind,
But you don't know where it comes from or where it is going.
Like an overflowing river, God goes left and right
Quenching our parched souls.
God caused the world to appear,
And keeps it from disappearing.
Yet God is discreet as if hiding,
Making no demands or commands.
Allowing us to follow or not.
Silly us, thinking we have a choice
To alter the very laws of existence.
As God is in all things
And hidden in our hearts,
God can be called small.
Since all things vanish into it

And it alone endures,
It can be called great.
The wise learn by imitating God.
Thus, the Godly ones seek to
Accomplish each small task with complete devotion,
As if it were the greatest of tasks,
With neither demand nor command.

COMMENTARY

God's Spirit is transformative and can be likened to the wind that moves freely and mysteriously. God is the source of life, creation, and sustenance, like an overflowing river that quenches our deepest needs. The passage beautifully captures the essence of God's omnipresence and discretion, inviting us to recognize God's hidden presence in all things, even within our hearts.

Jesus' teachings in the Bible support the concept of God's Spirit giving new life. In John 3:5-6, Jesus explains the necessity of being born of the Spirit to enter the Kingdom of God.

The analogy of the wind as a symbol of God's Spirit aligns with John 3:8, where Jesus compares the Spirit to the wind, blowing where it pleases. The passage acknowledges God's role as the Creator and Sustainer of the world. Colossians 1:16-17 affirms that all things were created through God and hold together in Him.

The notion of God's discretion and absence of demands or commands is reflected in the idea that God allows us to choose whether to follow Him or not, respecting our free will. This aligns with Acts 17:30, which states that God has overlooked the times of ignorance, allowing people to seek Him.

The concept of God being in all things finds support in Acts 17:28, where Paul declares that we live and move and have our being in God. The verse's call to imitate God resonates with Ephesians 5:1, urging believers to be imitators of God as beloved children.

The passage's emphasis on accomplishing small tasks with devotion, as if they were the greatest, echoes Colossians 3:23-24, encouraging believers to work heartily for the Lord.

This text captures the essence of God's Spirit, omnipresence, and discreet yet influential presence. It highlights the transformative power of God's Spirit, which gives new life, guides us like the wind, and encourages us to imitate God in every aspect of our lives. By reflecting on these biblical themes, we can deepen our understanding of God's presence and seek to live in devotion and alignment with God's will.

NEXT STEP

Find Greatness in the Small: Approach each task with complete devotion, recognizing that even seemingly small actions can be significant when done with love and integrity. Before beginning a task and after completing one, pause momentarily to offer a blessing. Whether big or small, offer your work as a service to the world.

CHAPTER 35

The Words of God Delight the Soul

"People usually consider walking on water or in thin air a miracle.
But I think the real miracle is not walking on water or thin air,
but walking on Earth."
Thich Nhat Hanh

Is Heaven some far-off place?
Heaven is all around us,
Although we cannot see it,
Although we cannot hear it,
Although it has no borders.
The Godly ones engage it.
They learn the ethos of Heaven,
By following The Way of the Lord.
Aligning themselves thus,
The people are drawn to them
Because the people know they will not be harmed
And can rest in peace and contentment
Music and good food delight the senses,
The words of God delight the soul.

Heaven is near and is accessible to those who align themselves with The Way. Heaven is not some distant or unreachable place but rather a spiritual reality surrounding us. While we may not perceive it with our physical senses or define its borders, the verse suggests that the presence of Heaven is tangible to the Godly ones who engage with it.

The idea of Heaven being around us aligns with the biblical teaching that physical boundaries do not limit God's presence. Acts 17:28 states, "For in him we live and move and have our being," affirming that God's presence encompasses all creation.

The notion that the Godly ones engage with Heaven by learning its ethos resonates with Jesus' teachings about seeking God's Kingdom and His righteousness in Matthew 6:33. By following The Way, we strive to align our lives with God's will and principles, bringing the reality of Heaven into our daily experiences.

The passage highlights the transformative power of aligning with Heaven, drawing others to the Godly ones. This aligns with Matthew 5:16, where Jesus encourages believers to let their light shine before others, attracting them to God's presence through righteous living.

The assurance that those who align with Heaven will find peace and contentment echoes Jesus' invitation in Matthew 11:28-30, where He promises rest for the weary and burdened through a relationship with Him.

Last, the verse draws a parallel between the delights of the senses, such as music and good food, and the soul's delight in the words of God. Psalm 19:7-10 highlights the transformative power of God's words, which bring joy, wisdom, and nourishment to the soul.

In conclusion, this chapter reminds us that Heaven is not a distant place but a present reality accessible to those who follow The Way. By engaging with Heaven, we experience peace, draw others to God's presence, and delight in God's words' transformative power. It encourages us to seek God's Kingdom within and around us, living in alignment with His will and principles to experience the joys of Heaven here and now.

NEXT STEP

Reflect on the Beatitudes: Not as a Sermon, but as a Vision Statement. A description of what life would be like if we practiced and lived into the concept of The Kingdom of Heaven on Earth.

CHAPTER 36

Gentleness Overcomes Strength

> "Tenderness and kindness are not signs of weakness and despair,
> but manifestations of strength and resolution."
> Kahlil Gibran

To breathe in,
We must first breathe out.
To take in the teachings of the Lord,
We must first let go of our childish ways.
To gain knowledge, we must learn something.
To attain wisdom, we must release something.
To gain riches, we must acquire something.
To enrich our souls, we must give something away.
This is the subtle Way of the Divine,
The path to our true nature.
Arrogance weakens us,
As humility strengthens us.
Rome was strong.
The Lord was meek.
Yet Rome fell,
And the Lord became eternal.
Thus, gentleness overcomes strength.
And the meek overcomes the strong.

As a fish taken out of water is distressed,
We become distressed
When we do not follow our true nature.

COMMENTARY

This passage captures profound spiritual truths using insightful analogies. It emphasizes the importance of balance, humility, and selflessness in our journey toward understanding the Divine and finding our true nature.

Breathing in and out symbolizes a rhythm of life, where receiving divine teachings requires letting go of our childish and immature ways. This idea resonates with the Bible, particularly in 1 Corinthians 13:11, where the Apostle Paul speaks of putting away childish ways as we grow in faith.

Pursuing knowledge and wisdom is presented as a process of learning and releasing. Proverbs 1:7 highlights that the fear of the Lord is the beginning of knowledge, while Proverbs 3:7 urges us not to be wise in our own eyes, emphasizing the importance of humility.

The notion of acquiring riches and enriching the soul by giving aligns with the biblical teaching of giving generously. Proverbs 11:24-25 speaks of blessings for the generous, and 2 Corinthians 9:6-8 encourages cheerful sharing to reap God's abundant grace.

Drawing a contrast between the fall of the mighty Rome and the eternal nature of the Lord, the passage reminds us that gentleness and humility triumph over arrogance and strength. This echoes Jesus' teaching in Matthew 5:5 about the blessedness of the meek and James 4:6, where God opposes the proud but gives grace to the humble.

The analogy of a distressed fish taken out of water illustrates the inner turmoil we experience when we stray from our true nature. This echoes the Psalmist's yearning for God's presence, as expressed in Psalm 42:1-2.

In summary, the passage offers a profound spiritual reflection on finding harmony with the Divine, embracing humility, and cultivating a giving heart. Its themes echo throughout the Bible, reinforcing the timeless wisdom of seeking God's ways and living in alignment with our true nature.

Contemplation of Nature: Spend time in nature and observe its harmony and balance. Reflect on how different elements coexist peacefully and how nature's meek and gentle aspects often overcome the strong and forceful. Let this contemplation inspire you to align with the subtle Way of the Divine.

Belish/Shutterstock.com

CHAPTER 37

The Essence of God Is Love

"The fruit of love is service,
which is compassion in action."
Mother Teresa

God's will is subtle.
It is not expressed through action.
Yet, nothing remains undone.
Acting on our will,
Much remains undone.
The Lord accepted the Father's will
In the Garden of Gethsemane.
If the leaders and the powerful
Followed in The Way,
The world would be transformed,
And the people would live in harmony and simplicity.
If the leaders and the powerful
Seek to exercise their own will,
They will be devoured by greed and desire.
It is better to be free from desire
And allow the world to steady itself.

COMMENTARY

This chapter asks us to align our will with God's subtle and divine plan. It emphasizes that much remains undone when we act according to our desires, and we may be consumed by greed and avarice. The ultimate example of surrendering to God's will is demonstrated in the Garden of Gethsemane, where Jesus, the Lord, accepted the Father's will despite the imminent suffering.

The verse echoes the Bible's teachings on surrendering to God's will and seeking harmony and simplicity. In Matthew 26:39, Jesus prays in the Garden of Gethsemane, saying, "My Father, if it be possible, let this cup pass from me; nevertheless, not as I will, but as you will." This exemplifies accepting God's plan even in the face of extraordinary challenges.

Proverbs 19:21 speaks of the sovereignty of God's will, stating, "Many are the plans in the mind of a man, but it is the purpose of the Lord that will stand." This verse aligns with the idea that God's will remains unchanged and that nothing remains undone when it is carried out.

The contrast between following The Way and seeking to exercise one's own will is depicted in various biblical passages. Micah 4:3 speaks of a transformed world where nations beat their weapons into tools of peace, reflecting harmony and unity under God's guidance.

In 1 Timothy 6:9-10, the dangers of pursuing personal desires and greed are warned against, as they can lead to ruin and destruction. Instead, Matthew 6:19-21 encourages seeking treasures in heaven rather than accumulating earthly possessions, promoting a life free from excessive desire.

In summary, this verse underscores the significance of surrendering to God's will, seeking harmony and simplicity in life, and avoiding the pitfalls of personal desires and greed. By following The Way, the world can be transformed, and people can live in peace and unity, aligning with God's divine plan for creation.

NEXT STEP

Examine Your Intentions: Regularly examine your intentions behind your actions and decisions. Are they driven by self-interest, greed, or personal ambitions? Seek to align your motives with your desire for the greater good and the welfare of others.

CHAPTER 38

The Essence of God Is Love

> "The simplest acts of kindness
> are far more powerful
> than a thousand heads bowing in prayer."
> Mahatma Gandhi

God does not have to cultivate love.

The essence of God is love.

God is patient. God is kind.

God does not envy, it does not boast, it is not proud.

God does not dishonor others, nor is it self-seeking.

God does not anger and forgives without limit.

God does not delight in evil but rejoices with the truth.

God always protects, always trusts, always hopes, always perseveres.

God never fails.

Thus, God exemplifies true virtue.

We fear we cannot emulate true virtue,

Although it is our true nature.

Thus, we try to prove our virtue

By standing and praying in the synagogues and street corners,

And straying from our true nature.

Therefore, when relative virtue becomes prevalent,

We cease to be kind for only kindness's sake.

When kindness is lost,
Benevolence arises.
When benevolence is lost,
Righteousness arises.
When righteousness is lost,
Social and religious teachings are imposed.
When these become corrupted,
Empty rituals and etiquette become essential.
When etiquette becomes the path
It is because we have forgotten
The simple ways of fairness and kindness.

Therefore, the Godly reject these partial virtues of the world,
And return to their Divine nature.
They concentrate on the profound,
Rather than the shallow,
The root rather than the husk,
The fruit rather than the flower.
Understanding their true nature,
They know what to accept and what to reject.

COMMENTARY

The essence of God's nature is love, as described through various qualities such as patience, kindness, forgiveness, and humility. God's love is unconditional and all-encompassing, never failing or wavering. God embodies true virtue, providing a perfect example for humanity to follow.

The verse also points out the human struggle to emulate true virtue despite it being our inherent nature. Often, people seek to prove their virtue through outward displays, such as public prayers or religious rituals, but this can lead them away from their genuine nature and foster relative virtues rather than absolute ones.

Drawing from the Bible, 1 Corinthians 13:4-7 perfectly aligns with the description of God's nature as patient, kind, not envious, not boastful, and not proud. It encapsulates God's love, which "always protects, always trusts, always hopes, always perseveres."

The passage highlights the consequences of losing sight of genuine kindness, leading to the rise of other virtues, such as benevolence and righteousness. It echoes Micah 6:8, which reminds us of God's desire for humanity: "He has shown you, O mortal, what is good. And what does the Lord require of you? To act justly, love mercy, and walk humbly with your God."

In contrast, when social and religious teachings deviate from their original intent and become corrupted, empty rituals and etiquette replace the essential values of fairness and kindness. This is akin to the Pharisees' actions, which Jesus criticized in Matthew 23:5, where they did things to be seen by others but neglected the weightier matters of justice, mercy, and faithfulness.

NEXT STEP

Choose the Profound Over the Shallow: Prioritize the values of fairness, kindness, and love over superficial or materialistic pursuits. Invest time and energy in nurturing meaningful relationships and acts of service. Please make a list of everything important to you, then order them.

CHAPTER 39

Better to Honor a River Rock Than a Golden Calf

"The Earth does not belong to us:
we belong to the Earth."
Marlee Matlin

Since the beginning of time,
There have been those that
Live in accord with The Way of God.
"For the Son of Man came not to be served but to serve."
Understanding the unity of God's work,
They are content to be humble
And seek their place in the whole.
Seeing the world thus,
They make use of the sun and the rain;
The Earth is stable beneath their feet;
And the valleys are made fertile.
Their eyes are set on building solid foundations,
And the leaders rule with compassion and justice.
There have also been those
Who choose to live in accord with only themselves.
Not understanding the connectedness of creation,
They dirty the sky,
Pollute the Earth,

Cause the valleys to be barren,
Set their eyes on gilded penthouses,
And their leaders rule with greed and hate.
Better to honor a river rock
Than a jade and gold calf.

COMMENTARY

It is suggested that there are two distinct ways of living—one in accord with The Way of God, embracing humility, unity, and compassion, and the other centered on self-interest, leading to greed and destruction. The verse emphasizes the timeless choice between following God's path of service and building solid foundations or pursuing selfish desires that harm creation.

The reference to "For the Son of Man came not to be served but to serve" (Mark 10:45) underscores the importance of servitude and selflessness as exemplified by Jesus. This verse highlights a foundational principle of Christian faith, promoting a life dedicated to serving others.

The individuals who live in harmony with God's way, understanding the unity of God's work, exhibit contentment in humility. This echoes biblical teachings on humility, such as Proverbs 22:4, "The reward for humility and fear of the Lord is riches and honor and life." Their attitude toward creation allows them to benefit from God's blessings, symbolized by the sun, rain, and fertile Earth, as seen in Matthew 5:45, where God makes the sun rise on the evil and the good and sends rain on the just and unjust.

On the other hand, those who live for themselves and fail to recognize the interconnectedness of creation harm the environment and society. This reflects the consequences of selfishness and lack of understanding of God's design for the world, as warned in passages like Proverbs 14:31, "Whoever oppresses a poor man insults his Maker, but he who is generous to the needy honors him."

The verse's closing statement, "Better to honor a river rock than a jade and gold calf," echoes the biblical warnings against idolatry, where people worship false gods and place value in material possessions. The Bible warns against such practices, as seen in Deuteronomy 4:16-18, condemning the making of idols.

In summary, this verse serves as a poignant reminder of the timeless choice between living in harmony with God's way or pursuing selfish interests. It draws from various biblical references to emphasize the importance of humility, compassion, and selfless service while cautioning against greed and idolatry. The verse encourages us to embrace a life that honors the interconnectedness of creation and seeks to build strong foundations by following God's plan.

NEXT STEP

Simplicity and Contentment: Embrace a lifestyle of simplicity and contentment, recognizing that excessive material pursuits often lead to greed and disregard for the environment. Focus on building solid foundations of love, compassion, and kindness in your relationships.

CHAPTER 40

God Is Infinite Possibility

"All possibilities are lined up
in the field of infinite possibilities.
It is pure potential."
Deepak Chopra

God created the universe out of nothing.
And it is destined to return to nothing.
God is the great creative force.
All of creation will return to God.
Even when there is nothing,
There is God.
Is God nothing?
God is the plane of infinite possibility.
So, God is something, even in the field of nothing.

COMMENTARY

At the heart of this contemplation lies the foundational truth that God, the ultimate Creator, brought the universe into existence, as attested in Genesis 1:1.

The notion that God exists even in the void is intriguing and aligned with biblical wisdom. The assertion that "Even when there is nothing, there is God" resonates with Psalm 139:7-8, "Where can I go from your Spirit? Where can I flee from your presence? If I go up to the heavens, you are there; if I make my bed in the depths, you are there." This verse affirms the omnipresence of God.

The question "Is God nothing?" prompts introspection, reminding us of God's transcendence beyond human understanding, as declared in Isaiah 55:8-9, "For my thoughts are not your thoughts, neither are your ways my ways, declares the Lord. As the heavens are higher than the Earth, so are my ways higher than your ways and my thoughts than your thoughts."

The analogy of God as the "plane of infinite possibility" mirrors the concept of God's sovereignty over creation, as expressed in Colossians 1:16-17, "For in him all things were created: things in heaven and on Earth, visible and invisible, whether thrones or powers or rulers or authorities; all things have been created through him and for him. He is before all things, and in him, all things hold together." This perspective recognizes that God's potential and presence persist even within nothingness.

In conclusion, this contemplative journey weaves through biblical threads of creation, transcendence, omnipresence, and sovereignty. It invites us to ponder the profound interplay between God's creative power and creation's destiny. Whether in existence or absence, God's nature remains an unchanging anchor, an eternal force that orchestrates the intricate symphony of the universe.

NEXT STEP

Embrace Your Creative Nature. Engage in activities that allow you to express yourself and tap into the infinite possibilities within you. Let it be a channel for connecting with God's creative force, whether it's art, writing, music, or any other form of creative expression.

CHAPTER 41

The Teachings of the Lord Are Radical

"The greatest enemy of knowledge is not ignorance,
it is the illusion of knowledge."
Stephen Hawking

When the selfless hear of The Gospel,
They immediately seek to embody it.
When the apathetic hear of The Gospel,
They may be curious but shrug their shoulders.
When the selfish hear of the Gospel,
They laugh at it and also the selfless.
If they did not laugh, it would not be The Gospel.
They laugh because it seems self-contradictory.
It is said:
The path to grace is full of suffering;
To gain community, we must give up family;
Those that are most rich are robed in beggar's clothing;
Those of the highest virtue are condemned with thieves;
Those that are most sure are the most easily shaken;
Great strength appears as weakness;
What is most accurate is the hardest to believe;
Profound words seem shallow;

What seems unfair is just, and
What is the law can be unjust.
The teachings of the Lord are Radical.
They call us to engage in a new paradigm.
His strong voice whispers.
His beauty is invisible.
He is the source and strength of all things.

COMMENTARY

Jesus' teachings are radical. When the selfless hear the Gospel, they immediately seek to embody its principles, reflecting the biblical call for us to be doers of the Word (James 1:22). Their selflessness aligns with biblical teachings on love, service, and putting others before oneself (Matthew 22:39, Mark 10:45).

In contrast, the apathetic response shows curiosity but a lack of commitment to wholeheartedly embracing the Gospel's message. This reflects Jesus' parable of the sower, where some seeds fall on rocky ground and do not take root (Matthew 13:5-6).

The selfish reaction to the Gospel is one of mockery and ridicule toward the selfless, echoing the scoffers and mockers described in the Bible who reject the truth (2 Peter 3:3). The verse suggests that the Gospel's self-contradictory, counterintuitive nature, like Jesus' call to self-denial for the sake of gaining true life (Mark 8:35), contributes to their laughter.

The verse further explores the paradoxical teachings of Jesus, such as the path to grace being full of suffering (Acts 14:22) and gaining community by giving up family (Matthew 10:37). It also emphasizes the inversion of values, where the richest are robed in beggar's clothing (Matthew 5:3), and the highest virtue may lead to condemnation with thieves (Luke 23:32-33).

The teachings of the Lord are described as radical, calling for a paradigm shift in how people perceive reality. It is as if He brought a new operating system to the world. The verse points out that profound truths may initially seem shallow, aligning with Jesus' use of parables to convey profound spiritual truths (Matthew 13:10-13).

Finally, the text acknowledges that Jesus, the source and strength of all things, communicates with a gentle, whispering voice (1 Kings 19:12). His beauty is invisible to the human eye (Isaiah 53:2). This verse invites readers to contemplate the profound mysteries and transformative power of the Gospel, prompting them to respond with humility, openness, and a willingness to embrace its radical call.

NEXT STEP

Embrace Paradox and Mystery: Acknowledge that the teachings of Jesus often contain paradoxes and profound mysteries. Embrace the tension between seemingly contradictory concepts and recognize that some truths may be hard to grasp fully. Allow these mysteries to deepen your faith.

CHAPTER 42

In the Beginning, There Was Only God

In the beginning, there was only God.
God created Man, and from Man, made Woman,
And woman gives birth to Man.
Thus, Man resides in Woman,
And Woman resides in Man.
God created the energy we call male.
God created the energy we call female.
He imbued man with the masculine energy
And the feminine energy,
So that man could understand woman.
He imbued woman with the feminine energy
And the masculine energy,
So that woman could understand man.
It was the combination of these energies
That populated the world,
And filled it with the 10,000 things.
The masculine energy accomplishes.
The feminine energy nurtures.
Too much masculine leads to war.

Too much feminine leads to la la kumbaya.
Balancing these energies leads to The Great Harmony.
When Harmony is lost, the people
Become lonely as orphans and widows,
And believe themselves to be unworthy.
Those who lead with harmony and balance
Understate their importance.
We hear them say:
It happened through me, not by me.
They are quick to give others credit.
Put all this aside.
The most essential teaching is this:
Those who live a violent life,
Shall not enjoy a natural death.

COMMENTARY

This teaching reflects on the interplay of masculine and feminine energies, their role in creation, and the importance of achieving harmony and balance in life. While not directly found in the Bible, the concepts resonate with some biblical principles.

In the beginning, there was only God. This echoes the biblical understanding of God as the Creator of all things (Genesis 1:1).

God Created Man and Woman: The creation of humanity as male and female is described in Genesis 1:27.

The Combination of Energies Populated the World: This idea aligns with the biblical principle of procreation and the continuation of life through human reproduction.

Masculine Energy Accomplishes, Feminine Energy Nurtures: The roles of men and women often reflect different strengths, and the Bible acknowledges complementary roles within families and societies (Ephesians 5:22-25).

Balancing Energies Leads to The Great Harmony: Achieving harmony and unity is central to biblical teachings (Colossians 3:14).

Loneliness and Unworthiness Without Harmony: The Bible addresses the importance of community and relationships and how isolation can lead to distress (Psalm 68:6).

Giving Others Credit and Understating Importance: The biblical principle of humility encourages acknowledging the value of others and not seeking self-glorification (Philippians 2:3).

The Teaching Against a Violent Life: The Bible promotes peace and condemns violence (Matthew 5:9).

While the specific combination of ideas and language may not be directly found in the Bible, the text reflects universal themes in biblical teachings. It emphasizes the significance of balance, harmony, humility, and peaceful living in a world created by God.

NEXT STEP

Examine Your Energies: Reflect on your energies and tendencies. Are there areas in your life where you lean too much toward masculine or feminine energy? Identify any imbalances and areas that need nurturing or accomplishment.

God created Man, and from Man, made Woman, And Woman gives birth to Man. Thus, Man resides in Woman, And Woman resides in Man.

The Tai Chi symbol above is the best-known symbol of Taoism. The dark represents Yin, the female energy. The light represents Yang, the male energy. The dark dot in the male energy is the seed of the female energy. As time passes, the seeds will bloom. Yang will become Yin, and Yin will become Yang. A representation of the ever-cycling Nature of the universe; day turns to night, summer turns to winter, good times and bad times also cycle.

CHAPTER 43

The Insubstantial Rules the Substantial

"Your beliefs become your thoughts, your thoughts become your words,
your words become your actions, your actions become your habits,
your habits become your values, your values become your destiny."
Mahatma Gandhi

Right and wrong are insubstantial,
Yet they are more important than the densest gold.
Love and hate cannot be held in the hand,
Yet they melt and forge cannons and swords.
Thus, the insubstantial rules the substantial.
He who had no substance
Entered that which had no openings.
His teachings are without words.
Everyone does not hear them.

COMMENTARY

The short yet profound chapter presents insights into the nature of moral values, emotions, and spiritual teachings. While the specific phrasing is not found in the Bible, the concepts are consistent with biblical principles.

Right and Wrong Transcend Material Worth: The verse suggests that right and wrong, being insubstantial, hold greater importance than the densest gold. The Bible emphasizes the value of wisdom and righteousness over material riches (Proverbs 8:10-11, Proverbs 16:16).

Love and Hate Shape Humanity: Love and hate are intangible emotions yet have significant consequences. The Bible encourages love as the central virtue (1 Corinthians 13:13) and warns against hatred and its destructive power (1 John 2:9-11).

The Insubstantial Rules the Substantial: The verse highlights that the immaterial aspects of life hold more significant sway. This aligns with the biblical principle that the spiritual realm influences the physical realm (Colossians 3:1, Ephesians 6:12).

He Who Has No Substance Enters into That Which Has No Openings: This enigmatic statement suggests that those who are humble and empty of self-importance can access profound truths. The Bible often reveals God's wisdom to the humble and contrite in the heart (Psalm 34:18, James 4:10).

His Teachings Are Without Words and Not Heard by Everyone: This part implies that true wisdom goes beyond verbal expressions and is not accessible to all. In the Bible, the Holy Spirit is said to teach and reveal spiritually discerned truths (1 Corinthians 2:10-14).

In summary, the verse conveys timeless truths about the importance of moral values, the power of emotions, the significance of spiritual wisdom, and the need for humility in understanding profound truths. Though not directly from the Bible, the concepts resonate with biblical teachings, guiding individuals to seek eternal truths beyond material possessions and to embrace the transformative power of love and righteousness.

NEXT STEP

Seek Understanding of Profound Truths: Recognize that some truths may not be immediately apparent to everyone. Be patient and open to the idea that deeper insights and spiritual understanding may require time and personal growth.

CHAPTER 44

Hoarding Is Like Being Clogged

> "Happiness is not in the mere possession of money;
> it lies in the joy of achievement,
> in the thrill of creative effort."
> Franklin D. Roosevelt

As for your fame and your life,
Which matters more?
As for money or happiness,
Which is more valuable?
Which brings more pain, success, or failure?
Are you a camel forcing yourself through the eye of a needle?
Whether it be money, possessions, or ideas,
Hoarding is like being constipated.
It fogs the mind.
How can counting your riches
And fearing their loss,
Compare to the treasures God has given freely?
To live a long and fruitful life
Take Paul's advice:
Learn to be content with whatever you have.
Better to bathe naked in the forest,
Than in a tub full of coins and gold.

The Bible teaches that life, knowing and obeying God, learning from success and failure, avoiding material hoarding, and finding contentment are more important than pursuing wealth or fame.

Fame and Life: The Bible teaches that life is more valuable than fame. In Mark 8:36, Jesus says, "For what does it profit a man to gain the whole world and forfeit his soul?"

Money or Happiness: The Bible teaches that true happiness comes from knowing and obeying God rather than material possessions or wealth. 1 Timothy 6:10 says, "For the love of money is a root of all evils. Through this craving, some have wandered away from the faith . . ."

Success or Failure: The Bible teaches that success and failure are part of life and that we should learn from both. James 1:2-4 says, "Count it all joy, my brothers, when you meet trials of various kinds, for you know that the testing of your faith produces steadfastness."

Hoarding: The Bible teaches that hoarding material possessions can harm our spiritual well-being. In Matthew 6:19-21, Jesus says, "Do not lay up for yourselves treasures on earth, . . . but lay up for yourselves treasures in heaven . . ."

Contentment: The Bible teaches that true contentment comes from being satisfied with what we have and being grateful to God for His blessings. In Philippians 4:11-13, Paul says, "I have learned in whatever situation I am to be content. . . .I can do all things through him who strengthens me."

NEXT STEP

Identify areas where you may be hoarding, whether material possessions, ideas, or unhealthy attachments. Practice letting go of physical and mental clutter to create space for clarity and peace of mind.

CHAPTER 45

Things Are Not as They Seem

> "The world is full of magic things,
> patiently waiting for our senses to grow sharper."
> W. B. Yeats

Things are not as they seem.
Science is beginning to discover
The workings of God.
If you set out on a journey
Of Ten Trillion miles,
You will return to the beginning.
What appears here in one moment,
Is there in the next, or not at all.
A tiny atom can power
Ten thousand homes.
A single dot in the night sky can house
Ten Billion stars.
Thus, for one not rooted in the Kingdom of Heaven,
The wisdom of the Lord
Falls aside the path, on rocks or thorns.
They are given great perfection,
Yet, they are left wanting.
They are exposed to great wisdom,

And are left confused.
Though seeing, they do not see,
Though hearing, they do not listen.
For those rooted in the Kingdom of Heaven
What seems crooked is straight.
What seems fragile, endures.
Stillness overcomes heat,
And activity relieves the chill.
They Know when to take action,
And when to stay calm.

COMMENTARY

This verse highlights the profound and often paradoxical nature of God's creation. It emphasizes that the true essence of reality goes beyond appearances and that science is merely beginning to uncover the intricacies of God's workings. The verse invites readers to contemplate the vastness and interconnectedness of the universe, where even a tiny atom can hold immense power, and a single dot in the night sky houses countless stars.

It contrasts the perspective of those not rooted in the Kingdom of Heaven with those who are spiritually grounded. For the former, the wisdom of the Lord may be missed, leading to confusion and a sense of lacking despite possessing excellent knowledge and accomplishments. On the other hand, those rooted in the Kingdom of Heaven see through the illusion of appearances. They understand the power of stillness amid chaos and know when to act and when to remain calm.

This verse resonates with biblical themes found in various passages. For instance, Proverbs 3:5-6 encourages trusting the Lord's wisdom rather than relying on human understanding. In Matthew 6:33, Jesus teaches to seek the Kingdom of Heaven and its righteousness first, acknowledging that everything else will fall into place. The verse also echoes Ecclesiastes 3:1, which speaks of the appointed times and seasons for various actions.

In summary, the verse urges readers to look beyond the surface and seek spiritual grounding in the Kingdom of Heaven, where they can find true wisdom, clarity, and understanding of life's complexities.

Surround Yourself with Like-Minded Individuals: Seek fellowship with others rooted in the Kingdom of Heaven. Engage in discussions and share insights to grow in spiritual understanding together.

When we follow the way of Heaven, we employ horses to till our fields. When we stray from the way of Heaven, we force horses to pull canons and give birth on the battlefield.

CHAPTER 46

Greed Begets Greed

"Greed is a bottomless pit that exhausts the person
in an endless effort to satisfy the need
without ever reaching satisfaction."
Erich Fromm

God created the world,
And the 10,000 things,
And gave us dominion over them.
When we follow the way of heaven,
We employ horses to till our fields.
When we stray from the way of heaven,
We force horses to pull canons
And give birth on the battlefield.
The greatest mistake a nation can make
Is to be covetous.
God's creatures bear the consequences
Of their self-centeredness.
The Lord warned us,
"Watch out! Be on your guard against all kinds of greed."
Greed begets greed,
And grows beyond the ability
Of any harvest to satisfy it.

Those who heed the Lord
Know when enough is enough,
And enjoy the satisfaction of being content.

COMMENTARY

This meditation speaks to the idea that God created the world and everything in it, and as human beings, we have been given dominion over His creation. When we follow the way of heaven, which aligns with God's will and principles, we use our resources wisely and responsibly. We treat His creatures with care and respect, using them for beneficial purposes, like tilling fields.

However, when we deviate from the path of righteousness and become self-centered and greedy, we misuse God's creation for destructive purposes, like employing horses to pull canons and engaging in warfare.

The Bible warns us against greed and covetousness, as it can lead to a never-ending cycle of desire, leading to more greed and dissatisfaction. Jesus, in Luke 12:15, cautions us to be on guard against all kinds of covetousness.

To live harmoniously with God's plan, we must cultivate contentment and recognize when we have enough. Proverbs 30:8-9 encourages us to ask God to provide what we need and to be content with just that so we don't fall into the trap of seeking more and more.

In summary, this verse emphasizes the importance of following God's way, being responsible stewards of His creation, and guarding against greed to find true satisfaction and contentment.

NEXT STEP

Reflect on Greed and Desire: Regularly reflect on the dangers of excessive desire and greed. Study passages that warn against the unhealthy pursuit of wealth and material possessions. This reflection can help you prioritize the values of simplicity and contentment.

CHAPTER 47

We Must Learn to Love Ourselves

"You can't hate yourself happy.
You can't criticize yourself thin.
You can't shame yourself worthy.
Real change begins with self-love and self-care."
Jessica Ortner

We are given two great commandments.
How do we accomplish this?
We are asked why we are preoccupied with
A speck of sawdust in our brother's eye,
Even as we pay no attention to the plank in our own eye?
If we are to love our neighbor as ourselves,
We must first learn how to love ourselves.
Are we not, each one of us
Also, a child of Abba, Father God?
All we need to know already resides within.
Without stepping outside the door,
We can comprehend the world.
Without glancing through the window,
We can see the landscape of heaven.
The more we seek wisdom in the hearts of others,
The less we know.

Missionaries listen well:
Sit at the feet of the Holy Spirit within
And be taught,
Before seeking to make disciples of all nations.

COMMENTARY

This passage emphasizes the two great commandments given to us: to love God with all our heart, soul, and mind and to love our neighbor as ourselves. It reminds us of the importance of self-reflection and self-love to love others truly. The analogy of the speck of sawdust and the plank in the eye warns against hypocrisy and urges us to examine ourselves before criticizing others. (Matthew 22:36-40, Matthew 7:3-5)

The verse highlights the idea that we are all children of God, and within each of us, God's wisdom resides. It encourages us to seek the divine wisdom within ourselves rather than solely relying on external sources. Looking inward, we can better understand the world and connect with the heavenly realm. (Romans 8:16, 1 Corinthians 3:16)

The passage advises missionaries and those seeking to spread the Gospel to first sit at the feet of the Holy Spirit within and be taught. It underscores the importance of personal spiritual growth and understanding before sharing teachings with others. (James 1:5, John 14:26)

NEXT STEP

Cultivate Self-Compassion: Recognize that each person is a child of God, including oneself. Practice self-compassion and self-love, understanding that a healthy self-love is a foundation for loving others.

CHAPTER 48

God's Plan Emerges from the Haze

Great teachers have said that from the beginning.
Find your heart, and you will find your way."
Carlos Barrios

We will never understand
The ten virgins, the ten bags of gold, the sheep, and the goats.
To become learned,
We must gain more knowledge every day.
To achieve wisdom,
We must let go of what we already know every day.
It is hard to be wise,
When you have too much to think about.
Let go, simplify, and deprogram.
With clarity and a quiet mind
God's plan emerges from the haze.
The timeline of the Universe is not our timeline.
Forcing our time on God's
Is like picking an unripe apple with the grinding of teeth,
And being left with a tart fruit.
Or waiting until it drops and rots.
Those attuned to God's time

Effortlessly pick ripe, sweet apples.
By interfering the least, the most is accomplished
By not tampering with the natural way
The world will heal itself
Those that meddle with God's creation
Are not fit to be leaders.

COMMENTARY

This reflection emphasizes the pursuit of wisdom through gaining knowledge and the need to let go of preconceived notions continually. Drawing inspiration from biblical parables such as the ten virgins, the ten bags of gold, and the sheep and the goats, the text encourages simplicity, clarity, and a quiet mind to discern God's plan.

The allusion to the parables reminds us of the importance of being prepared and faithful, like the wise virgins and the diligent servants who multiplied their talents. This calls for learning and gaining knowledge daily to achieve wisdom, as stated in Proverbs 1:7 and James 1:5.

Furthermore, letting go of what we already know aligns with Proverbs 3:5-6, where we are encouraged to trust the Lord and not lean on our understanding. By simplifying and deprogramming, we open ourselves to divine guidance and wisdom.

The imagery of picking a ripe, sweet apple with ease contrasts with the hardship of pulling a tart one with grinding teeth, symbolizing the benefits of aligning with God's timing and the consequences of straying from it.

The passage also emphasizes humility and noninterference with God's creation. By not tampering with the natural order, we recognize God's sovereignty and allow the world to heal itself. This concept resonates with Job 12:13-16, highlighting God's wisdom and might in His creation.

Ultimately, the text conveys a call for humility, trust in God's plan, and a continuous pursuit of wisdom through gaining knowledge while releasing preconceived notions. It reminds us that those who humbly follow God's guidance without interfering with His creation are best equipped to lead others with wisdom and understanding.

Journaling: Keep a journal to jot down your reflections and thoughts each day. Write about your experiences and challenges in letting go of preconceived notions, simplifying your life, and seeking clarity.

CHAPTER 49

Jesus Went Where He Was Called to Go

> "Do your little bit of good where you are;
> It's those little bits of good put together
> that overwhelm the world."
> Desmond Tutu

Jesus did not need preconceived ideas and plans.
He went where he was called to go.
And responded to what the world presented
From His integral nature.
He answered the people's questions,
As their concerns were his concerns.
He was good to those that are good,
And to those that are not good,
Because his very nature is good.
He was honest with those that were honest,
And with those who were not honest,
Because His very nature was virtue.
Not being concerned with worldly things,
He was one with the world.
People turned their eyes and ears to him
And he regarded them with the love
Parents have for their children.

COMMENTARY

These verses highlight various aspects of Jesus' character and how He responded to the world and people around Him. He exemplified humility, love, honesty, and virtue, showing us a perfect example to follow in our own lives.

This verse beautifully captures the essence of Jesus' character and his approach to life. It portrays Jesus as someone who embodied perfect wisdom, love, and virtue. Jesus' interactions with people throughout the Gospels exemplify his selfless and compassionate nature.

The verse highlights how Jesus didn't rely on preconceived ideas or plans but listened and responded to the needs and concerns of those around him. This aligns with biblical passages that emphasize the obedience of Jesus to God's will and his commitment to doing the Father's work (John 6:38, John 5:30).

Furthermore, Jesus' innate goodness and virtue allowed him to treat everyone with love and kindness, regardless of whether they were considered good. He exemplified loving one's enemies and turning the other cheek (Matthew 5:43-48).

Jesus' honesty and integrity are also showcased, as he spoke the truth and brought light to darkness. He demonstrated that He embodies truth (John 8:32, John 14:6).

The verse rightly points out that Jesus was not attached to worldly things but was one with the world profoundly and compassionately. He was approachable, and people turned to him with their questions and concerns, finding comfort and hope in his presence (Matthew 11:28).

In summary, this text encapsulates Jesus' divinely integral nature, his boundless love for humanity, and his willingness to be a guiding light in a broken world. It reminds us to seek wisdom and virtue in our lives, following the example set by Christ, who regarded others with the same love and care parents have for their children. As believers, we can draw inspiration from Jesus' selfless character and aspire to live with the same passion and compassion toward those around us.

NEXT STEP

Reduce Reactivity, Enhance Responsiveness: Notice knee-jerk reactions and assess their helpfulness. Pausing for just a few moments before reacting allows for responding more helpfully and constructively.

CHAPTER 50

One Out of Ten Follows the Lord

> Two roads diverged in a wood, and I—
> I took the one less traveled by,
> And that has made all the difference."
> Robert Frost

Life in the world begins at birth,
And ends in death.
Out of ten that are born,
One-third puts on the armor of the hard worker
To live a successful life that leaves much undone.
One-third puts on the armor of preoccupation with life and death
To live a life of radiance and perfection full of boogeymen and danger.
One-third put on the armor of the philanderer,
To live a life of pleasure full of desire, passion, and dissatisfaction.
The last of the ten follows in The Way,
And dons no armor at all.
He is what he appears to be.
As he has not presented a defense,
he poses no threat.
By lowering his shield,
he has become invulnerable.
He confuses the rhinoceroses, tigers, and soldiers among us.

They cannot find the crack to insert their horns, claws, or swords,
Because he has set his eyes on a purpose greater than himself.
He considers his body but an appendix.
He smiles as the courage of Esther washes over him.
"And if I perish, I shall perish."
And he was content,
As his life was peaceful and content.

COMMENTARY

This chapter presents a thought-provoking portrayal of different life paths that individuals may choose. It vividly depicts three distinct approaches to life, with the last one exemplifying the way of the Lord. This individual stands out by embracing vulnerability, selflessness, and a higher purpose, leading to contentment and peace. The verse echoes biblical principles found throughout the Scriptures, urging us to follow the way of self-sacrifice, love, and devotion to God's purpose.

The verse aligns with the teachings of Jesus, who encouraged his followers to deny themselves, take up their crosses, and follow Him (Matthew 16:24). It also resonates with the Apostle Paul's words about boasting in weaknesses, relying on God's strength in times of difficulty (2 Corinthians 12:9-10). The imagery of setting aside armor and lowering shields reflects the biblical call to trust in God's protection and guidance rather than relying on worldly defenses (Psalm 18:2, Ephesians 6:10-18).

Furthermore, the reference to Esther's courage and willingness to perish for a more significant cause echoes the biblical theme of finding courage in adversity and trusting in God's providence (Esther 4:16, Joshua 1:9). The pursuit of a purpose greater than oneself reflects the call to love God with all our heart, soul, and mind, and to love our neighbors as ourselves (Matthew 22:37-39).

This verse beautifully encapsulates the choice between self-centered pursuits and a life lived in The Way. Individuals can find peace, contentment, and a deeper connection with God by following the latter path, characterized by vulnerability, humility, and selflessness. The imagery of the invulnerable one confounding the threats around them echoes the power of a life grounded in faith and divine purpose.

Lay Down Defenses: Let go of the armor of self-protection and defensiveness. Open yourself to vulnerability. This may seem counterintuitive. Once we befriend our inner spirit, all we hide is our light. Drop your shields and become invulnerable. "What you see is what you get."

The Mystical Virtue of the Holy of Holies

> "The whole is greater than the sum of its parts."
> Aristotle

God gave birth to all things,
Both the Material and the Immaterial.
God created the Material so that things could be done.
God created the Immaterial to guide what things should be done.
God created the environment to feed, shelter, and grow the material.
God created the immaterial with virtue and love,
Along with greed and hate,
So that nature may sharpen itself on the opposition,
And good things are done.
"For just as the body without the spirit is dead,
So faith without works is also dead."
Imagine,
God gave birth to all things but does not possess them,
Helps all things but does not obligate them,
Guides all things but does not control them.
This is the mystical virtue,
Of the Holy of Holies.

This text offers a meditation on the biblical perspective of God's role in creation and the intricate relationship between the material and immaterial.

The verse begins with the assertion that "God gave birth to all things, both the Material and the Immaterial." Genesis 1:1 establishes this fundamental truth: "In the beginning, God created the heavens and the earth."

The idea that "God created the Material so things could be done" reflects the biblical concept of divine providence. Throughout the Bible, we find instances of God's provision for humanity's physical needs, such as food and shelter. Psalm 104:14-15 reflects this idea: "You cause the grass to grow for the livestock and plants for man to cultivate, that he may bring forth food from the earth."

Similarly, the notion that "God created the Immaterial to guide what things should be done" shows that God provides moral guidance through the spiritual realm. Proverbs 3:5-6 underscores this idea: "Trust in the Lord with all your heart and lean not on your understanding; in all your ways submit to him, and he will make your paths straight."

The verse also acknowledges the coexistence of virtue and vice in the immaterial realm, mirroring biblical teachings about the presence of good and evil in the world. Romans 12:9 reminds us of the importance of love and virtue: "Love must be sincere. Hate what is evil; cling to what is good."

The concept that "nature may sharpen itself on the opposition, and good things are done" reflects that trials and challenges can refine and strengthen faith and character. James 1:2-4 conveys this thought: "Consider it pure joy, my brothers and sisters, whenever you face trials of many kinds because you know that the testing of your faith produces perseverance."

The concluding passage refers to God's sovereignty and grace. It reflects the teaching that God guides and supports, allowing free will rather than imposing control or force. This concept aligns with passages like Philippians 2:13: "For it is God who works in you to will and to act to fulfill his good purpose."

This chapter contemplates biblical themes surrounding creation, providence, morality, and divine guidance. It underscores the profound mystery of God's interaction with the world and the essential role of faith and works, echoing James 2:26, "For just as the body without the spirit is dead, so faith without works is also dead."

It invites us to contemplate the depth of God's involvement in creation, where divine wisdom and human agency intersect, ultimately leading to the pursuit of goodness and virtue.

NEXT STEP

Gratitude and Reverence: Cultivate a sense of appreciation and reverence for God's creation. Take time to appreciate the beauty and intricacy of life's material and immaterial aspects. Acknowledge the Creator and recognize His wisdom in designing a world that allows growth, learning, and overcoming challenges.

CHAPTER 52

Turn Away from Godless Chatter

"In a controversy, the instant we feel anger,
we have already ceased striving for the truth
and have begun striving for ourselves."
Abraham J. Heschel

Like a mother eagle that stirs up its nest
And hovers over its young;
That spreads its wings to catch them
And carries them aloft,
Mother God knows we are,
But finite minds trying to describe the infinite.
Mother God, who gave birth to everything.
God manifesting as the Lord.
Teacher of teachers.
By learning the way of the Lord,
We may catch a glimpse of God.
For the Lord can teach nothing by Himself,
He can teach what he only sees through God.
Because whatever God does, the Lord also does.
For God loves the Lord and all God's children
And hides nothing from them.
Close your eyes and examine the light within.

Clarify the small and subtle,
By calling on the light of the world.
Turn away from godless chatter,
And the opposing ideas of what is falsely called knowledge.
Close your ears to those who have an unhealthy interest in
Controversies and quarrels about words
That result in envy, strife, and malicious talk.
Do not fall prey to evil suspicions and constant friction
Between people of corrupt minds who have been robbed of the truth.
Resist those who think that godliness is a means to financial gain,
As it is from you, they secretly seek to gain.
Hold fast to the teaching of the Lord.

COMMENTARY

This evocative chapter portrays God's nurturing and protective qualities, symbolized by a mother eagle caring for her young. The passage emphasizes the mystery of the infinite nature of God, which surpasses our finite understanding. It acknowledges God as the Creator of everything and manifests in the Lord, who serves as the ultimate Teacher. We can glimpse God's character and divine wisdom by learning The Way.

The verse echoes several biblical references, such as Deuteronomy 32:11, which compares God's care to an eagle's for its young. It acknowledges God's all-encompassing love and knowledge, revealed through Jesus as the manifestation of God on earth (Colossians 1:15, John 1:14).

The teaching of the Lord finds support in John 13:13-15, where Jesus demonstrates humility and instructs His disciples to follow His example. Moreover, the unity between God and the Lord is reminiscent of Jesus' statement in John 10:30, where He proclaims His oneness with the Father.

The verse encourages introspection and turning away from godless chatter and false knowledge. It aligns with biblical teachings, urging us to seek the light within, which is Christ Himself (John 8:12). The passage also echoes Paul's exhortation to Timothy to avoid irrelevant discussions and controversies that distract from the truth (1 Timothy 6:20-21).

Lastly, the call to hold fast to the teaching of the Lord corresponds to numerous biblical passages emphasizing the importance of following God's commands and remaining steadfast in faith (John 14:23, Colossians 2:6-7).

In essence, this verse encapsulates God's nurturing care and wisdom, guiding us to seek the light of Christ, turn away from distractions, and firmly embrace the Lord's teachings in our faith journey.

NEXT STEP

Meditate on Mother God's Nurturing Nature: Take time to reflect on God's nurturing and protective qualities, symbolized by a mother eagle. Visualize yourself under God's caring wings, knowing God is always watching you with love and guidance.

CHAPTER 53

The Vanity of Robbers

"The test of our progress is not whether we add more
to the abundance of those who have much;
it is whether we provide enough for those who have too little."
Franklin D. Roosevelt

If I had a scintilla of sense,
I would sit at the feet of the Lord and drink in His teaching.
I would learn the way of the Lord.
It is a smooth and wide path,
Yet many are lured away from it
By promises of power and wealth.
When the people are not united in the value of The Way,
Their leaders become divided;
The fields become overgrown;
And the granaries are empty.
Some have gorgeous garments, carry sharp swords,
And feast on food and drink.
While others fret over paying the rent or their medicine
This is called the vanity of robbers.
That some are enriched, while some are hard-pressed
Is not The Way of the Lord.

This teaching reflects on the importance of seeking wisdom and guidance from the Lord and the consequences of straying from His path. It acknowledges the value of sitting at the feet of the Lord, learning His ways, and embracing the smooth and wide path of righteousness. However, the passage also highlights the allure of worldly temptations, such as power and wealth, which can lead people astray.

The verse emphasizes the impact of unity or division among the people on their leaders and society. When the value of "The Way" is not upheld collectively, leaders become divided, and the community suffers with overgrown fields and empty granaries. The imagery of some indulging in luxury while others struggle to meet basic needs depicts the inequality and injustice that result from selfish pursuits.

In line with biblical principles, the verse points out the vanity of worldly pursuits that prioritize personal gain over the welfare of others (Matthew 6:19-21, James 1:27). It echoes the call to seek first the kingdom of God and His righteousness (Matthew 6:33) and reminds us of the biblical teaching of caring for the less fortunate and oppressed (James 2:15-17).

Overall, the verse serves as a thoughtful reflection on the significance of seeking divine wisdom, staying on the path of righteousness, and living in unity with values prioritizing justice and compassion for all. It urges readers to embrace God's ways and strive for a society where the well-being of all is valued and cared for.

NEXT STEP

Hold Leaders Accountable: Participate actively in civic life and hold leaders accountable to uphold values that align with these teachings. Advocate for just policies and actions that benefit the entire community. Be an Ambassador for the greater good.

CHAPTER 54

Bring The Way into Your Life

> "Be the change that you wish to see in the world."
> Mahatma Gandhi

Once The Way of Christ is well established,
It cannot be uprooted.
Once The Way is firmly held,
It cannot be stolen.
Parents, plant deeply The Way in your children.
They will thrive,
As will their children's children,
And they will be known by the fruit they bear.
When The Way is cultivated in oneself,
One becomes authentic.
When cultivated in the home,
The family will flourish.
When The Way is cultivated in the community,
The community becomes supportive.
When cultivated in the nation,
The nation becomes an example for all Nations.
When The Way is enabled in the world,
It becomes the culture of the land,

When cultivated in the Universe,
The Universe sings.
Therefore, one can see that one influences the family.
The family influences the community.
The community influences the nation.
And the nation influences the world.
Therefore, bring The Way into your life,
And it will spread all about you.
How do I know this is true?
Because I have seen The Way move and live.

COMMENTARY

Embracing The Way has a transformative power that can have a cascading effect on individuals, families, communities, nations, and even the entire world. The teaching emphasizes the importance of nurturing and deepening one's faith in Christ, which results in flourishing and authenticity. The verse also emphasizes the responsibility of parents to pass down the values of The Way to future generations, leading to a legacy of fruitful lives.

The concept of "The Way" aligns with Jesus' teachings about following Him and living in alignment with God's will (John 14:6). The verse highlights the significance of establishing a firm foundation in Christ, which cannot be uprooted or stolen, symbolizing the security and stability that comes from faith in Jesus.

The biblical principles of sowing and reaping (Galatians 6:7) resonate with the idea that those who deeply plant The Way in their lives will see the fruit of their faithfulness in the generations to come. It also echoes the call to be the salt and light of the world, influencing and positively impacting those around us (Matthew 5:13-16).

The verse beautifully emphasizes the interconnectedness of individuals and their communities. Cultivating The Way at every level, from personal lives to entire nations and the world, brings about positive transformation and reflects God's goodness and love.

In conclusion, this verse exudes a profound sense of hope and encouragement, inspiring readers to embrace The Way of Christ wholeheartedly, recognizing its potential to influence and transform not only their lives but also the lives of others, ultimately impacting the world for good.

NEXT STEP

Be a Role Model: Be aware that you are, in fact, a role model, whether for the helpful or for the harmful. As parents, grandparents, or mentors, model The Way in your life. Demonstrate love, kindness, and integrity to those around you, especially the younger generation.

fizkes/Shutterstock.com

CHAPTER 55

Accept the Stages of Life with Grace

"To be yourself in a world
that is constantly trying to make you something else
is the greatest accomplishment."
Ralph Waldo Emerson

And Jesus said, "Let the little children come to me,
And do not hinder them,
For the Kingdom of God belongs to such as these.
Honestly, I tell you,
Anyone who will not receive the Kingdom of God
Like a little child will never enter it."
Look at the newborn babe.
It is the embodiment
Of innocence, of wholeness.
It is pure potential,
An uncarved block.
The entire village will protect it.
Its bones are tender, its muscles soft, yet its grip is firm.
It has not known the union of male and female,
Yet when joyful, it is as if it was newly in love,
Not with one person,
But with all creation.

It can howl and scream all day long,
Without becoming hoarse.
Their bodies seem relaxed and pliant,
But their stamina and strength are remarkable.
This is because the baby does what babies do.
If the people want to enter the Kingdom of Heaven,
They must live their lives as babies do.
They must develop a strong back,
And a soft heart.
They must experience the union of male and female,
Only in joy and innocence
Eat when hungry, sleep when tired.
Live neither in excess nor paucity.
Take the gifts of life with gratitude.
Accept the stages of life with grace,
And be in harmony with them.
Just as breath is a natural function
And forcing it through the will of the mind
Only serves to exhaust the spirit,
To pretend to be what one is not
Violates the authenticity of the child.
This is called arrogance,
And is not the path to the Kingdom.

COMMENTARY

This verse from Mark 10:14-15 presents a profound teaching by Jesus about the significance of childlike qualities in entering the Kingdom of God. Jesus warmly welcomes little children, exemplifying their innocence and trust as attributes that lead to the Kingdom of God. He stresses that only those who receive the Kingdom with the heart of a little child will be able to enter it.

The verse's essence aligns with Jesus' teaching on humility. In Matthew 18:3-4, He says, "Truly I tell you, unless you change and become like little children, you will never enter the kingdom of heaven. Therefore, whoever takes the lowly position of this child is the greatest in the kingdom of heaven." The commentary reinforces this idea by emphasizing the need for a "soft heart" and experiencing the union of male and female "in joy and innocence," stressing the importance of purity and humility.

The depiction of a newborn's qualities as "pure potential" and an "uncarved block" resonates with the biblical concept of rebirth. In John 3:5, Jesus tells Nicodemus, "Truly, truly, I say to you, unless one is born of water and the Spirit, he cannot enter the kingdom of God." Just as a baby represents new beginnings, spiritual rebirth is crucial for entering the Kingdom.

The commentary's message to "live neither in excess nor paucity" reflects the biblical principle of contentment, emphasized by the Apostle Paul in Philippians 4:12-13, "I know how to be brought low, and I know how to abound. In any and every circumstance, I have learned the secret of facing plenty and hunger, abundance and need. I can do all things through him who strengthens me."

The warning against pretending to be what one is not and its association with arrogance aligns with the Bible's warnings against hypocrisy. Jesus often rebuked religious leaders for their hypocrisy, emphasizing the need for authenticity in one's faith.

In conclusion, this commentary beautifully elaborates on the timeless wisdom in Jesus' words about childlike qualities and their significance in entering the Kingdom of God. It emphasizes humility, purity, authenticity, and contentment as vital attributes for those seeking a deeper spiritual connection with God. The subsequent reflection on the newborn babe expands on this teaching, drawing parallels between the characteristics of a baby and the virtues required to inherit the Kingdom of Heaven.

A newborn's innocence, wholeness, and untapped potential illustrate the purity and openness we should maintain in our relationship with God. Like the newborn's grip, we should hold on firmly to our faith in God yet remain receptive to His guidance with tender and soft hearts.

NEXT STEP

Cultivate Childlike Qualities: Reflect on the childlike qualities mentioned in the passage, such as innocence, trust, joy, and openness. Embrace these qualities in your approach to faith, relationships, and life. Nurture a sense of wonder and curiosity like a child.

CHAPTER 56

I May Lay Down in Green Pastures

> "Peace comes from within. Do not seek it without."
> Buddha

Those that understand the message of the Christ,
Do not need to preach.
For their very lives and acts are their words.
Those that are confused by the message of the Christ,
Babble on and on
Pretending to know what they are unsure about.
I will accept the Lord as my Shepherd.
I will place guardians at the portals to my mind,
So that I may lay down in green pastures
And be restored by the still waters within.
Those who learn The Way
Shut the doors to useless noise.
Their integrity is quiet.
They blunt the sharp barbs,
Untangle the knots,
Dim the dazzling lights,
And know that in the end,
They will return to the dust

From which they arose.
This is called being anointed.
Comforted by His rod and His staff,
They feel neither lacking nor neglected,
So can be neither seduced nor abandoned.
They feel neither flawed nor proud.
So, can be neither honored nor humiliated.
Asking for little and giving much,
Leading with integrity,
Following with loyalty,
They are the most esteemed and revered in the world.

COMMENTARY

The chapter and reflection present a commentary on the understanding and embodiment of the message of Christ. It contrasts those who genuinely grasp the essence of Christ's teachings with those who are confused and merely parrot empty words. The passage emphasizes the significance of living out the message of Christ through one's actions and lifestyle rather than relying solely on verbal preaching.

The reference to accepting the Lord as a Shepherd, as found in Psalm 23:1, exemplifies trust and reliance on God's guidance, leading to peace and restoration. By guarding the portals of the mind, individuals create a space of tranquility where they can find solace in the presence of God, symbolized by green pastures and still waters.

The concept of "The Way," possibly inspired by Jesus' statement in John 14:6, highlights the path of truth and righteousness we should follow. It advocates for the silence of useless noise and the cultivation of quiet integrity, reflecting the fruit of the Spirit as described in Galatians 5:22-23.

The idea of returning to dust, reminiscent of Genesis 3:19, signifies the recognition of human mortality and the transient nature of life. This realization is not met with fear but with a sense of being anointed and comforted by God's guidance and protection, as mentioned in Psalm 23:3-4.

In summary, the commentary underscores the importance of genuine understanding and embodiment of Christ's teachings in one's life. It encourages believers to live with humility, integrity, and loyalty, finding contentment in their relationship with God and thereby gaining honor and esteem in the eyes of the world. The reflection serves as a reminder that true discipleship involves living out the message of Christ through love, compassion, and righteous actions, thus becoming a living testimony to His transformative power.

NEXT STEP

Guard Your Mind: Be mindful of the information and influences you allow into your mind. Protect yourself from unnecessary noise and distractions that can lead to confusion. Surround yourself with positive, uplifting content that aligns with The Way.

CHAPTER 57

The Godly Leader Practices Self-Reflection

"He who has not learned the power of sincere and selfless contribution,
lacks the very essence of leadership."
John C. Maxwell

To govern a people,
Justice is an admirable goal.
If war must be waged,
Make good use of surprise.
To win the world,
Only the will of God must prevail.
When the leaders are not transformed
By their self-reflection,
When they cease to examine their desire,
So that they may discern
What is the will of God,
So that they may discern
What is good and acceptable and perfect
They fall prey to their own will and desire.
They impose more prohibitions and restrictions,
And the people become poorer.
The more weapons they buy,
The more people are insecure.

If they are cunning and clever,
Chaos reigns in the land.
The more laws and regulations they pass,
The more thieves and robbers thrive.
Therefore, the Godly ruler practices self-examination,
Casts out his desire
And pledges to execute God's will.
She becomes peaceful,
And the people are at peace.
She intervenes the least,
And the people rise to the task themselves.
She remains quiet,
And the people are not confused.
She does not revere silver and gold,
And the people return to the simple ways of the Lord.

COMMENTARY

The verse reflects a wisdom about just governance and the qualities of a righteous leader. While the specific verse is not found in the Bible, its themes resonate with biblical principles and teachings.

The concept of justice as an admirable goal aligns with various passages in the Bible. Micah 6:8 emphasizes the importance of acting justly and walking humbly with God. Proverbs 20:18 advises planning with wise guidance in the context of war, which could be related to good use of surprise in warfare.

Romans 12:2 teaches about self-reflection and the need for transformation by renewing the mind to discern God's will. Following God's will echoes Romans 12:2 and is also seen in the prayer of Jesus in the Garden of Gethsemane (Luke 22:42).

The passage warns about the dangers of leaders falling prey to their own will and desire, reminiscent of biblical accounts of leaders who allowed their passions to lead them astray, such as King David's affair with Bathsheba.

The idea of a Godly ruler practicing self-examination and seeking to execute God's will resonates with the humble leadership of biblical figures like Moses and King Solomon. The call for leaders to be peaceful and not revere silver and gold aligns with biblical teachings on humility and not prioritizing worldly possessions.

While the specific verse is not directly from the Bible, the themes of just governance, self-examination, and following God's will can be seen throughout the Scriptures. The passage serves as a reminder for leaders to govern with humility, seek God's wisdom, and ensure the well-being of their people.

NEXT STEP

Self-Reflection: Engage in a regular, authentic, disciplined practice of self-examination and introspection to understand your desires and motivations. Be honest with yourself and seek to align your intentions with what is just, trustworthy, and kind.

CHAPTER 58

Both Good and Evil Inhabit the Earth

"The function of prayer is not to influence God,
but rather to change the nature of the one who prays."
Søren Kierkegaard

If the Sabbath is enforced
To control the people,
The people are discontent and cunning.
If the Sabbath is used
To heal the people,
The people are healthy and at ease.
Did not Rome rule with power and force,
Yet it is the meek that shall inherit the earth.
Both good and evil inhabit the earth.
It is in the struggle between them,
That we see the changes in life.
What is proper today,
May become improper tomorrow.
What is helpful today,
May become harmful tomorrow.
What serves as justice today,
May become unjust tomorrow
Who knows the explanation of things?

A person's wisdom brightens their face
And changes its hard appearance.
God opposes the proud
But shows favor to the humble.
Therefore, those that follow The Way.
Have firm principles and are just
Without judging.
Are honest without being hurtful.
Guide without regulating.
Serve as an example and model,
Without forcing others to be as they are.
They are brilliant,
Without being dazzling.

COMMENTARY

The teaching reflects on the significance of intention and approach in governance and leadership, drawing parallels between enforcing control and promoting healing and humility.

The idea that enforcing the Sabbath to control people leads to discontent and cunning resonates with the Gospel accounts of Jesus rebuking religious leaders for burdening the people with excessive legalistic interpretations of the Sabbath (Matthew 23:4). In contrast, using the Sabbath to heal and restore aligns with Jesus' compassionate healing ministry on the Sabbath (Matthew 12:10-13).

The reference to the meek inheriting the earth echoes Jesus' teaching in the Sermon on the Mount (Matthew 5:5) and is a recurring theme throughout Scripture (Psalm 37:11).

The passage acknowledges the presence of good and evil in the world and the ever-changing nature of human affairs (Ecclesiastes 3:1-8). It underscores the humility required to navigate life's uncertainties, which finds biblical support in passages like James 4:6 and 1 Peter 5:5, where God opposes the proud but favors the humble.

The emphasis on following the way of the Lord with firm principles and without judgment aligns with Jesus' teaching to love others and to be an example of godly character (Matthew 5:43-48).

While not directly from the Bible, the verse reflects a wisdom consistent with biblical teachings on leadership, humility, and compassion. It serves as a reminder of the transformative power of genuine care for people's well-being and the importance of humility in leadership. By emulating the qualities of those who follow the way of the Lord, individuals can shine with a brilliance that comes not from dazzling displays of power but from a humble heart devoted to serving others.

NEXT STEP

Be Adaptable and Open-Minded: Recognize that circumstances change, and what may be proper or helpful today might not be so tomorrow. Be adaptable and open-minded to navigate life's uncertainties. There is little benefit to holding onto a procedure merely because "That's how we have always done it."

CHAPTER 59

There Is No Greater Mandate than Moderation

"Example is not the main thing in influencing others.
It is the only thing."
Albert Schweitzer

In guiding others, serving Heaven,
And leading your own life,
There is no greater mandate than moderation.
It is not good to eat much honey,
Nor is it glorious to seek one's glory.
Many things may be lawful,
But not all are helpful.
Acting excessively enslaves us.
Show yourself in all respects to be a model of good works,
And in your teaching, show integrity and dignity.
Be sober-minded: Be watchful.
There are many harmful forces about
Seeking to devour someone.
Get right with God.
"For nothing will be impossible with God."
If you walk The Way of the Lord
There is nothing you can't do,

Even change the course of history.
Therefore, be imitators of God as beloved children.
Set your roots deep and build a firm foundation.
Let your reasonableness be known to everyone.
The Lord is at hand.

COMMENTARY

Moderation and righteousness are important in guiding others and leading one's own life.

The first reference is from Proverbs 25:27, "It is not good to eat much honey, nor is it glorious to seek one's own glory." This verse warns against indulgence and self-centeredness, urging us to avoid excessive desires that may lead to negative consequences.

The second reference is from 1 Corinthians 6:12, "Everything is permissible for me, but not everything is beneficial. Everything is permissible for me, but I will not be mastered by anything." Here, the focus is on understanding that while certain things may be lawful, they may not be beneficial or lead to true freedom. Acting excessively can enslave us and hinder our spiritual growth.

The third reference comes from Titus 2:7-8, "Show yourself in all respects to be a model of good works, and in your teaching show integrity, dignity." This verse highlights the importance of leading by example and living a life of virtue.

The fourth reference draws from 1 Peter 5:8, "Be sober-minded: be watchful. Your adversary, the devil, prowls around like a roaring lion, seeking someone to devour." It reminds us to be vigilant against harmful forces and temptations that may lead us astray.

The fifth reference is from Luke 1:37, "For nothing will be impossible with God." This verse underscores the power of faith and reliance on God, acknowledging that we can achieve great things and change the course of history through Him.

The final reference is from Ephesians 5:1-2, "Therefore, be imitators of God, as beloved children. And walk in love, as Christ loved us and gave himself up for us, a fragrant offering and sacrifice to God." This verse encourages us to emulate God's character and love, reflecting His nature in our actions and relationships.

In summary, the commentary emphasizes the significance of moderation, righteousness, and faith in guiding others and leading a purposeful life. By embodying these principles, we can set a positive example and have a transformative impact on the world.

NEXT STEP

Develop a Morning Reflection: Begin each day with a positive affirmation based on a verse that can remind you of your commitment throughout the day. Start with something simple and build it over time. You are trading a day of your life for whatever you may leave in the day. Let it be something good.

CHAPTER 60

Governing a Country Is Like Frying a Small Fish

> "The devil doesn't come dressed in a red cape and pointy horns.
> He comes as everything you've ever wished for."
> Tucker Max

Governing a country and disciplining the mind
Are both like frying a small fish.
With too much poking and turning
It will fall apart,
And the bones will mix with the meat.
Both evil and good exist in the hearts of people.
They vie for control of the soul.
The one that gets more attention,
Will flourish.
If anyone returns evil for good,
Evil will not depart from his house.
Submit yourselves, therefore, to God.
Resist the devil,
And he will flee from you.

COMMENTARY

This chapter draws a vivid comparison between governing a country and disciplining the mind, likening them to frying a small fish. Just as excessive poking and turning while frying the fish leads to its disintegration, overthinking and constant agitation of the mind can cause mental fragmentation and turmoil.

The verse acknowledges the coexistence of good and evil within the human heart. It highlights the perpetual struggle between these opposing forces as they vie for control of the soul. What receives more attention and focus within us will ultimately flourish and shape our character and actions.

The principle of sowing and reaping is underscored, warning against returning evil for good. The consequences of such actions will linger and affect one's household, as seen in Proverbs 17:13.

The verse concludes with a call to submission to God and resistance against the devil, as found in James 4:7. Surrendering to God's guidance and resisting the temptations of evil leads to spiritual growth and inner peace.

This verse offers valuable insights into wise governance and mental well-being. It urges us to maintain a balanced leadership approach and discipline our thoughts, avoiding excessive negativity and turmoil. Focusing on goodness, submitting to God, and resisting evil can cultivate peace, righteousness and positively impact our lives and the world around us.

NEXT STEP

Balanced Decision-Making: Embrace the analogy of governing a country and apply it to decision-making. Practice a balanced approach, avoiding impulsivity or excessive interference. Take the time to consider different perspectives and consequences before making choices.

Governing a country and disciplining the mind are like frying a small fish. With too much poking and turning, it will fall apart, and the bones will mix with the meat.

CHAPTER 61

Every Conqueror Eventually Falls

"When I despair, I remember that all through history
The Way of truth and love have always won.
There have been tyrants and murderers, and for a time,
they can seem invincible, but in the end, they always fall.
Think of it—always."
Mahatma Gandhi

The Lord humbled himself,
And thus was exalted by God.
The Nation of Israel Chose Worldly Power
Over the advice and counsel of God.
Thus, the people and the nation
Chose arrogance over humility.
In the long run,
This has not served their purpose.
Every conqueror eventually falls.
If a large nation
Wants the friendship of a small nation,
It must be a friend.
If a small nation
Wants the company of a large nation,
It also must be a friend.

Enduring relationships
Between people and nations
Are based on mutual respect and humility,
Not on swords and cannons.
The Kingdom of God
Offers grace, love, and the fruits of the spirit
To all nations.
It does not force itself on any.
Therefore, if a great nation follows The Way,
All it wants is to spread its resources to its neighboring nations.
If a small country follows The Way,
All it wants to do is apply those resources
To the benefit of the people.
Thus, each gets what it wants,
But only with humility and submitting
To The Way of the Lord.

COMMENTARY

This verse emphasizes the importance of humility and submission to God's way, drawing from various biblical principles. It begins by highlighting how the Lord exemplified humility, and through that, He was exalted by God (Philippians 2:8-9). In contrast, the people of Israel, in their pursuit of worldly power and self-proclaimed chosen status, chose arrogance over humility, ultimately leading to adverse consequences.

In the Old Testament books of 1 Samuel and 2 Samuel, the Israelites ask for a king to rule over them like the other nations, despite God's warnings about the potential consequences of having a human king. This desire for worldly power and a human king over God's guidance ultimately leads to the anointing of Saul as the first king of Israel. Saul's reign was marked by conflict, threat, and contention.

The verse underscores the notion that lasting relationships between individuals and nations are founded on mutual respect and humility (Philippians 2:3). It admonishes both large and small nations to seek friendship by being friendly themselves, not through coercion or force.

The Kingdom of God stands in stark contrast to the methods of the world. Without imposition, it offers all nations grace, love, and the fruits of the Spirit (Galatians 5:22-23). The verse conveys that if a great nation follows The Way, it desires to spread resources for the benefit of neighboring nations. Likewise, if a small country follows The Way, it seeks to apply resources for the betterment of its people. The key to fulfilling these desires lies in humility and submission to the ways of the Lord.

Essentially, the verse serves as a reminder that genuine strength and lasting prosperity come not through arrogance and dominance but through humility, respect, and adherence to God's principles. By embracing humility and submitting to God's way, individuals and nations can find true fulfillment and achieve harmonious relationships based on mutual understanding, respect, and cooperation.

NEXT STEP

Embrace Forgiveness: Study forgiveness and learn what forgiveness is and what it is not. Let go of grudges and relieve yourself of the victim mindset. This act of humility might not mend broken relationships and promote reconciliation, but it will relieve you of a heavy burden.

CHAPTER 62

The Kingdom of Heaven Resides in the Heart

"The heart is the place where we live our passions.
It is frail and easily broken but wonderfully resilient.
There is no point in trying to deceive the heart.
It depends upon our honesty for its survival."
Leo Buscagli

The Kingdom of Heaven is vast.
It is the source of all that is.
It spreads its love in equal measure.
It causes the Sun to rise on the evil and the good,
And sends rain on both the just and the unjust.
Where, then, is this Kingdom?
You can go to the four corners of the eight directions,
You can go to the edge of the universe,
Or to the depths of the seven seas,
You can look among clever words and good deeds,
It is there; it is everywhere.
Yet you will not find a scrap of sod
To stand on.
It resides in the heart.
Therefore, if ever given the occasion
To offer gifts to new leaders and their ministers,

You might flatter them with jade and stallions,
But to truly honor them,
Sit with them in the silence of the soul.
Help them to open their hearts
To The Way,
And to enter The Kingdom of Heaven.

COMMENTARY

The chapter captures the essence of the Kingdom of Heaven as a vast, all-encompassing source of love and abundance. It draws inspiration from several biblical references, emphasizing the inclusive nature of divine love. The imagery of the sun rising on both the evil and the good and the rain falling on the just and unjust (Matthew 5:45) exemplifies how the Kingdom's love is bestowed upon all without discrimination.

The verse reflects on the search for the Kingdom of Heaven, inviting us to explore every corner of the universe yet acknowledging that it cannot be physically located. Instead, it resides within the heart, emphasizing the spiritual nature of this divine realm (Luke 17:20-21). The verse encourages readers to seek the Kingdom within themselves and recognize the divine presence in their hearts and souls.

The final part of the text offers wisdom for interacting with leaders and ministers. While it is customary to offer material gifts and compliments, the true way to honor them is to help them connect with their inner selves and open their hearts to the teachings of the Lord. This approach aligns with Jesus' teachings, as he often emphasized the importance of spiritual transformation and the inner life (Matthew 15:8, Matthew 23:25-26).

In conclusion, the verse and commentary serve as a reminder of the boundless and inclusive love of the Kingdom of Heaven. It prompts us to seek this divine realm within ourselves and approach leadership focusing on spiritual growth and genuine connection. By doing so, we can become ambassadors of the Kingdom, spreading love, compassion, and understanding to the world around us.

Meaningful Conversations: Engage in meaningful conversations with others about the teachings of The Way. Share its message of love and inclusivity with friends, family, or like-minded communities. Discuss how these teachings can be applied in everyday life and inspire positive societal change.

CHAPTER 63

Meet the Difficult While It Is Easy

"By failing to prepare, you are preparing to fail."
Benjamin Franklin

The Lord,
The Son of Man
Prayed for things both big and small.
He gave his love and attention to everything and everyone.
Nothing was unimportant to Him.
He returned animosity with virtue
Because He understood the deeper truth.
He went to mountains and deserts to commune with God,
And contemplate his actions
Because he knew the importance of his purpose.
When He met with three temptations in the wilderness,
He was steadied and prepared as he knew they were coming.
Thus, He dealt with big issues
While they were still small.
When Satan tempted Him,
He was quick to respond without hesitation,
His replies at hand.
He acted without deliberation because he dealt with the difficult,
While it was easy.

Therefore, those who follow in The Way
Prepare themselves for challenges before being challenged.
Meet the difficult while it is easy.
Meet the big while it is small.
The most difficult in the world,
Is easy in its beginning.
Lightly given promises are met with little trust.
Taking things lightly can lead to losing the Way.
Therefore, those who follow in The Way,
Know how to remove Oak Trees when they are sprouts.
They are attentive.
They are not indifferent.
They see difficulty as it arises,
And thus avoid trouble.

COMMENTARY

The reflection portrays the Lord, the Son of Man, as a profound model of wisdom and spiritual insight. It highlights His devotion to prayer, love for everything and everyone, and ability to handle challenges with readiness and virtue. This portrayal finds resonance in various biblical references, illuminating the qualities of Jesus as a compassionate and wise leader.

In Matthew 6:9-13, we find the Lord's Prayer, showcasing Jesus' emphasis on both big and small concerns in prayer. His all-encompassing love is reflected in Matthew 22:37-39, where He instructs us to love God and our neighbor with all one's heart. The concept of returning animosity with virtue echoes Romans 12:21, encouraging overcoming evil with good.

The verse's depiction of Jesus retreating to mountains and deserts to commune with God aligns with instances in the Gospels where Jesus sought solitude for prayer (e.g., Mark 1:35, Luke 6:12). His encounter with three temptations in the wilderness (Matthew 4:1-11) demonstrates His preparedness to confront challenges.

The call to deal with big issues while still small resonates with biblical wisdom, as seen in Proverbs 22:3, which advises prudence in foreseeing and avoiding potential problems. The passage also echoes Jesus' swift responses to Satan's temptations during His forty days in the wilderness.

The text emphasizes vigilance and attentiveness to avoid difficulties, mirroring Jesus' teachings in Matthew 26:41 to watch and pray to not fall into temptation.

Overall, the verse artfully weaves biblical principles and references, showcasing Jesus as a model of spiritual insight and inviting followers to embrace wisdom, love, and preparedness in navigating life's challenges.

NEXT STEP

Mindful Response to Challenges: Embrace the idea of dealing with big issues while they are still small. When faced with challenges, take a mindful approach by pausing, acknowledging the difficulty, and reflecting on potential solutions before responding. Draw inspiration from Jesus' preparedness when He encountered temptations in the wilderness.

CHAPTER 64

Trust in the Will of the Father

"Faith is to believe what you do not see;
The reward of this faith is to see what you believe."
Saint Augustine

Those who are deeply rooted in The Way
Easily nurture their souls.
When they step off the path,
They quickly adjust to regain The Way.
They swiftly apologize.
And do not let insults or wounds fester.
The Lord offered different lessons
To the rulers and the ruled.
He was flexible and fitting.
For to be brittle is to be easily broken.
Both In the desert and in Gethsemane,
The Lord trusted in the will of the Father,
Despite temptation, torture, and death.
What are they like,
Those who trust in the will of the Father?
They organize complex matters when they are simple.
They act in faith,
Before things become unmanageable.

They do not rush heedlessly into things,
Nor lose attention as projects end
Because they are aware of the sanctity of their mission.
They do not take setbacks personally,
As they labor for something greater than themselves.
They do not desire accolades or self-glorification,
As they give all glory to the Father.
Those who follow their own will
Often ruin things on the cusp of success
Because their ego drives them to force completion.
Those that follow the will of the Father
Rely on their faith to balance their passion.

COMMENTARY

This verse encapsulates the virtues of being deeply rooted in The Way and trusting His will. It emphasizes the importance of humility, flexibility, and faith in navigating life's challenges and fulfilling one's purpose.

Being deeply rooted in The Way and efficiently nurturing the soul aligns with Psalm 1:1-3, which portrays the blessedness of those who delight in the law of the Lord, being like fruitful trees.

The emphasis on quickly adjusting and apologizing when one steps off the path reflects the biblical principle of repentance and seeking forgiveness, as mentioned in 1 John 1:9.

The example of the Lord offering different lessons to rulers and the ruled echoes Jesus' approach in adapting His teachings to diverse audiences, as shown in His parables and interactions with people from all walks of life.

The mention of the Lord's trust in the Father's will despite trials and suffering resonates with Jesus' surrendering to God's plan, as seen in His prayers in the desert (Matthew 4:1-11) and in Gethsemane (Matthew 26:36-46).

The passage encourages a life characterized by faith, humility, and purpose, aligning with biblical exhortations to act in faith (James 1:6-8), seek God's will (Proverbs 3:5-6), and work for the glory of God (Colossians 3:23-24).

The contrast between those who follow the will of the Father and those who pursue their own will echoes the biblical wisdom of seeking God's guidance and not leaning on one's understanding (Proverbs 3:5-6).

Finally, the verse offers a commentary on the virtues of being deeply rooted in The Way of the Lord and trusting in His will. It draws inspiration from various biblical references, encouraging believers to cultivate faith, humility, and a steadfast commitment to God's purpose. By following the way of the Father, individuals can navigate life's challenges with grace and find fulfillment in laboring for something greater than themselves, ultimately giving all glory to God.

NEXT STEP

Daily Self-Check: Throughout the day, periodically check in with yourself to ensure you are aligning your actions with the principles presented in the verse. Ask yourself if you are nurturing your soul, being flexible in your interactions, and adjusting quickly when you veer off the right path.

CHAPTER 65

It's Not So Helpful to Be Too Smart

"To know that you do not know is the best.
To pretend to know when you do not know is a disease."
Lao Tzu

In teaching the Way
The Lord confused those who knew,
And taught those who did not know.
The Pharisees were closed to the Lord,
While the meek were open.
When the people think they know
They are difficult to guide.
When all they know is the mystery,
They can become enlightened.
When leaning on your own understanding
The Lord cannot make your path straight.
Christ did not teach
The pursuit of earthly wealth and power,
But instead to wash feet.
Those that show The Way of Christ
Follow God's Divine Providence.
They trust in His abundance and grace.

In surrender and humility,
They find true peace.
As they rest in His love,
All worries and fears cease.

COMMENTARY

This chapter presents a commentary on the teachings of the Lord, highlighting the contrast between the receptive and the closed-minded, the enlightened and the self-reliant. It emphasizes the importance of humility, surrender, and trust in God's providence, as demonstrated through Christ's teachings and actions. The passage draws inspiration from various biblical references to convey its spiritual message.

The concept of the Lord confusing those who thought they knew and teaching those who were open aligns with Jesus' use of parables to convey spiritual truths to receptive hearts, as mentioned in Matthew 13:10-15. The Pharisees' closed-mindedness is exemplified in Matthew 23:13-15, while the blessedness of the meek is emphasized in Matthew 5:5.

The verse encourages avoiding arrogance in thinking one knows everything, as seen in Proverbs 3:5-6, which advises against leaning on one's understanding but instead trusting in the Lord's guidance. It also acknowledges the potential for enlightenment when embracing the mystery, which resonates with seeking spiritual wisdom through faith in God's mysteries.

Regarding Christ's teachings, the verse contrasts pursuing earthly wealth and power with the humble act of washing feet, as illustrated in John 13:12-15, where Jesus sets an example of selfless service. The call to follow God's Divine Providence, trusting in His abundance and grace, aligns with Matthew 6:25-34, where Jesus teaches not to worry about material needs but to trust in God's care.

The conclusion emphasizes finding true peace through surrender and humility, echoing Philippians 4:6-7, where believers are encouraged to present their requests to God with thanksgiving, finding peace that surpasses understanding.

In summary, this verse beautifully encapsulates the essence of Christ's teachings and the significance of humility, surrender, and trust in God's providence. It draws upon various biblical references to convey its spiritual insights, reminding believers to follow The Way and experience true peace by resting in His love and grace.

NEXT STEP

Adaptability in Lessons: Embrace a flexible approach to learning and teaching. Like all the great wisdom teachers, be adaptable in offering lessons to different individuals according to their needs and understanding.

CHAPTER 66

The Lord Is Called Master Because He Leads by Serving

"True leaders understand that leadership
is not about them but about those they serve.
It is not about exalting themselves, but about lifting others up."
Sheri L. Dew

Rivers and streams flow.
There is power and utility in their current,
Yet it is the sea that sits below them
That is the trustworthy source of their power.
How strong would the river be
If it divorced itself from the sea?
Those who lead others in The Way
Know that the people
Are the children of the sea.
Those who become great
Surrender their glory to service.
They do nothing out of selfish ambition,
Or vain conceit.
They value others above themselves.
They embrace humility with a sense of urgency.
Their devotion is high.

But the people do not resent them.
Their force is strong,
But the people are not oppressed.
They have food and clothing,
Take enjoyment in their toil,
And are content,
Because they do not compete with others.
They do not waste energy on defending themselves.
They live in the joy of their simplicity.

COMMENTARY

This insight creatively uses the imagery of rivers and streams flowing into the sea to illustrate a profound spiritual message. It highlights the significance of humility, selflessness, and contentment in those who lead others in The Way. While the exact wording is not verbatim in the Bible, the concepts presented align with various biblical principles.

The comparison of rivers and streams finding their true power and utility in the sea relates to the biblical truth that our strength and purpose come from being connected to God, who is the ultimate source of power and guidance (Psalm 46:1). This metaphor emphasizes the importance of staying rooted in God's presence to fulfill our potential.

The idea that those who become great surrender their glory to service reflects the teachings of Jesus, who exemplified servant leadership (Mark 10:43-45). Surrendering selfish ambitions and valuing others above oneself aligns with Paul's exhortation in Philippians 2:3-4.

The verse also conveys contentment and simplicity, reflecting Paul's teaching in 1 Timothy 6:6-8 on godliness with joy and the value of being satisfied with the necessities of life.

The verse beautifully encapsulates essential biblical principles, encouraging believers to remain connected to God, lead with humility and service, and find contentment and joy in simplicity. By embracing these truths, individuals can experience a meaningful and purposeful life in The Way, as exemplified by the teachings and actions of Jesus Christ.

Practice of Feet-Washing: Symbolically practice feet-washing as an act of humility and service to others. This can be a literal act of washing someone's feet or a symbolic gesture of serving others selflessly and humbly.

oksana.perkins/Shutterstock.com

CHAPTER 67

Three Treasures

> "A good leader takes a little more than his share of the blame,
> a little less than his share of the credit."
> Arnold H. Glasow

The people say,
"God is so powerful, so immense, It is inconceivable."
The wise are comfortable in the mystery.
The unwise force their conceptions upon God,
And lose their access to the power of God.
Because the wise trust the mystery,
They teach themselves
Simplicity, Kindness, and Humility.
Being simple, they do not worry about what they wear,
Thus, they can be generous.
Being kind, they know what heals,
Thus, they can be courageous.
Being humble, they are effective counselors,
Therefore, they can lead without corruption.
Following The Way,
They serve others before themselves.
Courage without compassion,

Generosity without moderation,
Leadership without humility,
Are banes to the world,
And lead to destruction.
Be simple, kind, and humble.
Be willing to heal on the Sabbath.
Let go of the myriad of laws and rules.
Follow the two great commandments.

COMMENTARY

This verse conveys profound spiritual wisdom, emphasizing the significance of embracing the mystery of God and cultivating qualities such as simplicity, kindness, and humility. It draws upon biblical principles to underscore the contrast between the wise and the unwise in their approach to God and life.

The notion that God's power and immensity are inconceivable aligns with the biblical understanding of God's transcendence and greatness, as stated in Isaiah 55:8-9. The verse reminds us that the wise are comfortable accepting the mystery of God's ways, as emphasized in Romans 11:33, where Paul marvels at the depth of God's wisdom and knowledge.

The call to be simple, not worrying about what to wear, echoes Jesus' teaching in Matthew 6:25-34, encouraging trust in God's provision. The emphasis on kindness and knowing what heals reflects the biblical principle of love and compassion, as seen in Mark 12:31 and James 5:16.

The verse also highlights the importance of humility in leadership, as exemplified by Jesus Himself in Matthew 20:25-28. The call to serve others before oneself aligns with Jesus' teaching in Mark 10:43-45, emphasizing servant leadership.

Additionally, the verse warns against courage without compassion, generosity without moderation, and leadership without humility, which resonates with the biblical exhortation to exercise virtues in balance and with Christ-like character.

The final call to be willing to heal on the Sabbath and to follow the two great commandments (Matthew 22:36-40) reminds us of the priority of compassion and love in our actions.

Overall, the verse beautifully weaves biblical principles, guiding us to embrace the mystery of God's ways, cultivate virtuous qualities, and prioritize love and compassion in our interactions with others. By embodying these teachings, we can experience a more profound and meaningful connection with God and live out His Way.

NEXT STEP

Noncompetitive Spirit: Avoid engaging in unnecessary competition with others. Instead, focus on personal growth and development, understanding that each person has their unique path and purpose.

CHAPTER 68

The Virtue of Noncontending

> "Darkness cannot drive out darkness;
> Only light can do that.
> Hate cannot drive out hate;
> Only love can do that."
> Martin Luther King Jr.

Jesus taught:
Turn the other cheek;
Love Your Neighbor;
Love your enemy.
Yet he confronted
The money changers,
The oppression of Rome,
The Laws of the Pharisees,
Without fear or force.
He was fully engaged yet accepted the results.
He confronted yet did not compete.
He challenged yet did not contend.
How is this possible?
It is because He did not stand for Himself,
But for all of the Father's creation.
Standing for what is greater than yourself,

Is to stand for justice and the Kingdom of God.
Humankind has created games
To learn how to be fully engaged,
Without becoming attached.

COMMENTARY

The teachings and actions of Jesus are paradoxical. They emphasize the principles of love, nonviolence, and standing for justice. He presented the world with a new paradigm to live out of.

In Matthew 5:39, Jesus teaches in the Sermon on the Mount that if someone slaps you on the right cheek, turn the other cheek to them. In Mark 12:31, Jesus declares that the second greatest commandment is to love your neighbor as yourself. In Matthew 5:44, Jesus instructs His followers to love their enemies and pray for those who persecute them. In Matthew 21:12-13, Jesus drives out the money changers and merchants from the temple, expressing His righteous anger against their exploitation of the sacred space. He challenged oppression and the laws of the Pharisees when, in Matthew 23:13-36 he offered a scathing rebuke of the Pharisees' hypocrisy and oppressive practices.

The text explains Jesus' approach to confronting injustice and evil. Despite challenging those who distorted God's purposes, Jesus remained unattached to personal gain or glory. He exemplified perfect love, seeking the greater good for all of God's creation and standing for justice and the Kingdom of God.

The concept of learning to be fully engaged without becoming attached reflects the biblical call to set our hearts on heavenly things (Colossians 3:2) and not be conformed to the patterns of the world (Romans 12:2). With slight playfulness, the verse ends by suggesting that we can learn about being engaged without being attached in the way we play games.

In summary, this verse celebrates the balanced and transformative character of Jesus, encouraging us to follow His example of selfless love, nonviolence, and standing for what is greater than ourselves—the Kingdom of God. By integrating these teachings into our lives, we can become agents of positive change, seeking justice and embodying the Way of Jesus in our interactions with the world.

Defend Only When Necessary: Be selective about defending yourself. Only engage in self-defense when it is essential for maintaining your integrity and standing up for truth and justice.

CHAPTER 69

War Is an Abomination

"War does not determine who is right—only who is left."
Bertrand Russell

The very essence of Christ
Teaches that war is an abomination,
And should be avoided.
The Godly arm themselves to avoid war.
The worldly arm themselves to enrich themselves.
The Godly battle with wisdom for justice
The worldly battle with anger for silver and gold
Goliath challenged the Israelites for 40 days.
Saul waited until the time and the purpose
Were aligned with God's will,
And then David responded.
There is no better expression of this
Then these words of Gandhi:
"When I despair,
I remember that throughout history,
The way of truth and love has always won.
There have been tyrants and murderers,
And for a time, they can seem invincible.

But in the end, they always fall.
Think of it—always."
The greatest mistake in battle is to dehumanize your enemy,
And thus be wounded by the loss of the three great treasures:
Love, Faith, and Hope

COMMENTARY

This verse encapsulates the essence of Christ's teachings by contrasting the ways of the godly with those of the worldly, drawing upon biblical wisdom and historical examples.

In Matthew 5:9 and Romans 12:18, the Bible underscores the importance of peacemakers and living in harmony with others, aligning with the idea that Christ's very essence teaches that war is an abomination and should be avoided. Proverbs 2:6 and Proverbs 21:31 indicate that the godly arm themselves with wisdom to pursue justice, while the worldly arm themselves for selfish gain.

The story of David and Goliath in 1 Samuel 17:45 illustrates waiting for the alignment of time and purpose with God's will before responding to challenges. This patience and divine alignment are essential aspects of the godly path.

The verse echoes the sentiments of Mahatma Gandhi, emphasizing the enduring triumph of truth and love throughout history, as seen in Romans 12:21 and 1 Corinthians 13:13. It reminds us that even tyrants eventually fall.

Perhaps the most profound message is in Matthew 5:44, where Jesus teaches us to love our enemies. The verse warns against dehumanizing our adversaries, as doing so causes us to lose the invaluable treasures of love, faith, and hope, as suggested in the final citation.

In essence, this commentary illuminates how Christ's teachings, supported by biblical references and historical wisdom, emphasize the importance of love, wisdom, and patience in pursuing justice and peace while cautioning against the dehumanization of others in any conflict.

Learning from History: Educate yourself about historical figures like Gandhi and their contributions to nonviolent movements. Study the success stories of nonviolent resistance and their lasting impact on society.

CHAPTER 70

The Teachings Are Easier Said Than Done

> "The quieter you become, the more you can hear."
> Ram Dass

The words of the Lord are easy to understand,
And easy to put into practice.
Love your God
With all your heart, soul, and mind.
Love your neighbor,
As yourself.
Yet the words are not understood,
Nor put into practice.
If you want to understand Christ,
First, understand his words.
Settle the chatter in your mind!
Love yourself as the Father loves you!
Then, the words will become clear.
If you want to understand the Lord,
First, look inside your heart.

The chapter reflects on the apparent simplicity of the Lord's teachings—notably the commandments to love God with all one's being and to love one's neighbor as oneself. These commandments are indeed easy to comprehend on a surface level, but the verse acknowledges that they are often challenging to grasp and put into practice fully.

The verse echoes the sentiments found in the Bible, where Jesus emphasizes the importance of love and understanding in living a righteous life. In Matthew 22:37-39, Jesus teaches the two greatest commandments: to love God with all one's heart, soul, and mind and to love one's neighbor as oneself. While these words may seem straightforward, the verse acknowledges that many struggle to comprehend and live by them genuinely.

The verse advises delving deeper into His words and teachings to understand Christ. Settling the chatter in one's mind implies finding inner peace and clarity through meditation and introspection. Loving oneself as the Father loves us aligns with Jesus' teachings on self-compassion and recognizing our worth as children of God (John 15:9-10).

The verse points out that understanding the Lord requires looking inside one's heart. This echoes Jesus' emphasis on purity of heart in Matthew 5:8 and the significance of obedience to God's commands in John 14:23.

Essentially, the verse urges us to move beyond a surface-level understanding of God's words and instead seek a more profound connection through love, introspection, and inner peace. By aligning our hearts and minds with Christ's teachings, we can better comprehend and practice the profound simplicity of His words, leading us to a more fulfilling and Christ-like life.

NEXT STEP

Understand What Meditation Is: Many think meditation is about emptying the mind. It is not. Meditation is the process of watching our thoughts flow through the mind from the nonjudgmental perspective of an observer. Seek out a learned meditation coach.

CHAPTER 71

Knowing That You Know Is Not Knowing

> "The more you know, the more you realize you don't know."
> Aristotle

God is unknowable and beyond understanding.
Those who know they do not know God,
Are wise and have health.
Those who say they know God,
Do not even know that they do not know.
For they have created God in their own image,
And this is sick.
The Lord shunned those who claimed to know.
And gathered to him the ones who yearned to learn,
Because they knew they did not know.
Because they recognized their faults,
They drew close to the one without fault.

COMMENTARY

This verse emphasizes the incomprehensible nature of God and the importance of humility in approaching the divine. The first part declares that God is beyond human understanding and knowledge. This concept aligns with various passages in the Bible, such as Isaiah 55:8-9 and Job 11:7-9, which emphasize that God's thoughts and ways are higher and deeper than our own.

The verse contrasts two groups of people regarding their understanding of God. The wise acknowledge their limitations in comprehending God's infinite nature. This idea aligns with Proverbs 1:7, which states that the fear of the Lord is the beginning of knowledge. Humility in recognizing our limitations allows us to draw closer to God and gain true wisdom.

On the other hand, the verse critiques those who claim to know God but have created Him in their own image. This notion parallels with warnings found in the Bible, such as Matthew 23:12, that exalting oneself and being prideful leads to God's opposition.

The verse implies that Jesus, during His time on Earth, sought those who humbly yearned to learn, like the tax collector in Luke 18:9-14. The Lord shunned those who boasted of knowing God without recognizing their faults.

In summary, this verse highlights the importance of humility and self-awareness in our relationship with God. Acknowledging our limitations in understanding the divine and recognizing our faults draws us closer to God's grace and wisdom. Those who approach God with a humble heart and a desire to learn are the ones whom the Lord embraces. Conversely, the verse critiques the arrogance of those who claim knowledge of God but fail to grasp His true nature. It serves as a reminder to seek God with a humble spirit, embracing the mystery of the divine while seeking His wisdom and truth.

NEXT STEP

Seek Wisdom from Others: Engage in conversations with individuals with different beliefs and perspectives about God. Listen and learn from their insights, fostering a more nuanced understanding of the divine.

CHAPTER 72

Embody Awe

"The best remedy for those who are afraid, lonely, or unhappy is to go outside,
somewhere where they can be quiet, alone with the heavens, nature, and God.
Because only then does one feel that all is as it should be."
Anne Frank

Awe in the Lord is the beginning of wisdom.
When the people lose their sense of Awe,
The Love of the Lord
Devolves into the trappings of politics and religion,
And disaster.
Those who lead with the awe of the Lord,
Do not intrude in the homes of the people.
They understand their talent,
But do not boast about their abilities.
They cherish themselves,
But do not worship themselves.
Thus, they reject the one and embrace the other.
They are the same for all,
Such is the value of the awe-filled leader.

COMMENTARY

This caution offers profound insights into the role of reverence for the Lord in pursuing wisdom and ethical leadership. The verse begins with a direct reference to Psalm 111, which declares that awe in the Lord is the foundational principle of wisdom. This citation establishes the core theme of the verse—the centrality of awe in spiritual and moral understanding.

Continuing, the verse warns about the consequences of losing our sense of awe in the divine. It suggests that without this awe, the love of the Lord can degenerate into mere politics and religion, potentially leading to calamity. This aligns with the ethical teachings of Jesus found in Matthew 7:12, where he advocates treating others as we would like to be treated, emphasizing the importance of genuine love.

The verse describes the characteristics of leaders rooted in the Lord's awe. They are portrayed as individuals who respect the privacy and boundaries of others, a concept reflected in Matthew 7:12, fostering harmonious relationships within society. Furthermore, the verse draws on the wisdom of Proverbs 27:2, urging these leaders to acknowledge the talents of others without arrogant boasting about their abilities. This resonates with the biblical virtue of humility.

The verse then introduces the notion of self-worth and humility derived from 1 Corinthians 6:19, suggesting that awe-filled leaders cherish themselves without falling into self-worship. This echoes Jesus' teachings in Luke 14:11, where humility is a virtue. The concluding reference to Galatians 3:28 underscores the idea that leaders grounded in awe treat all individuals equally, transcending divisions and prejudices, which promotes inclusivity and unity.

NEXT STEP

Avoid Being Consumed by Politics and Religion: Avoid letting political ideologies or religious practices overshadow your genuine love for creation. Focus on fostering a personal relationship with the divine rather than getting caught up in external trappings.

Sakura Image Inc/Shutterstock.com

CHAPTER 73

God's Plan

> "The world has enough for everyone's needs,
> but not enough for everyone's greed."
> Mahatma Gandhi

The Subtle Way of Heaven
Gave birth to a world of peace and order.
The courage to oppose The Way
Brings chaos.
The courage to align with The Way
Brings harmony.
If the people go hungry,
It is not due to a lack of food.
It is due to the hoarding of abundance.
Did not Jesus feed the multitudes
With but the five loaves?
The Law of Heaven is like a giant web,
Although sparsely knit,
Nothing can slip through.
"Vocatusatque Non Vocatus,
Deus Aderit."*

*"Biden Or Not Biden, God Attends." Stone plaque at the entrance to the home of Carl Jung

COMMENTARY

The verse portrays the Subtle Way of Heaven as the world's source of peace and order. It highlights the consequences of opposing or aligning with this divine way. Those who courageously oppose it bring chaos, while those who embrace it bring harmony. The verse draws attention to the issue of scarcity amidst abundance, attributing hunger not to the lack of food but to the hoarding of resources. The reference to Jesus feeding the multitudes with five loaves and two fish exemplifies God's provision and abundance. The Law of Heaven is depicted as an all-encompassing web, ensuring nothing slips through its intricate design. The Latin phrase "Vocatusatque non vocatus, Deus aderit" signifies God's omnipresence, whether called upon or not.

The idea of the Subtle Way of Heaven aligns with the biblical concept of God's sovereignty and divine plan. Psalm 119:89-91 highlights the steadfastness of God's word and His ordering of the universe. The consequences of opposing or embracing God's way are reflected in verses like Isaiah 48:22, where there is no peace for the wicked, and Romans 12:18, which urges living in harmony with others.

The notion of abundant provision amidst scarcity parallels the story of Jesus feeding the multitudes with five loaves and two fish (Matthew 14:13-21). The Law of Heaven as an all-encompassing web corresponds to biblical ideas of God's wisdom and all-encompassing knowledge (Psalm 147:4-5).

In conclusion, while the verse lacks specific biblical references, its themes harmonize with biblical principles of God's sovereignty, provision, wisdom, and the consequences of opposing or aligning with His divine way. The verse urges us to courageously embrace the Subtle Way of Heaven, trusting in God's guidance, and finding harmony and abundance amidst chaos and scarcity.

NEXT STEP

Practice Courageous Alignment: When faced with decisions or situations, summon the courage to align with The Way, which brings harmony. This may involve making choices based on values of compassion, kindness, and empathy rather than self-interest or the desire for power.

CHAPTER 74

Life and Death

> "Death is not the greatest loss in life.
> The greatest loss is what dies inside us while we live."
> Norman Cousins

"Thou shalt not kill."
Is this not clear?
Perhaps there is a need for further clarification.
"Love your enemies."
"Do not resist an evil person."
"Do not repay anyone evil for evil."
"Beloved, never avenge yourselves,"
But leave room for the wrath of God."
The Lord went even further,
He counseled not only against destroying the body,
But also not to kill another's hope, spirit, or faith.
People live their lives fearing death,
Would it not be better to live loving life?
In God's creation,
There is a time to live and a time to die.
Thus, God appointed Nature
As the official executioner.
To have the arrogance

To substitute oneself for Nature
Is like a child seeking to cut wood
With the tools of a Master Carpenter.
All that will be left
Is ruined wood
And wounded hands.

COMMENTARY

The chapter reflects on the commandment "Thou shalt not kill" and its broader implications for living a life of love, compassion, and nonviolence. It highlights the need for further clarification on the commandment, provided through additional Bible teachings.

The verse references multiple biblical passages that underscore the importance of love, forgiveness, and nonretaliation. "Love your enemies" is found in Matthew 5:44, where Jesus teaches us to love and pray for those who persecute us. "Do not resist an evil person" and "Do not repay anyone evil for evil" are from Matthew 5:39 and Romans 12:17, respectively, where Jesus and Paul encourage a nonviolent response to wrongdoing.

The verse also points to the biblical teaching in Romans 12:19, which advises not to take revenge but to leave room for God's wrath. This aligns with the principle of not avenging oneself and trusting in divine justice.

Furthermore, the verse highlights Jesus' more profound counsel, which goes beyond physical killing to not destroy others' hope, spirit, or faith. This concept is rooted in Jesus' teachings about preserving the soul and treating others with love and respect.

The verse concludes by recognizing God's appointed time for life and death, echoing the wisdom of Ecclesiastes 3:1-2. It warns against arrogance in substituting oneself for God's providence, emphasizing trust in His divine plan.

In summary, the verse calls for embracing the commandment against killing and expanding it to encompass love, forgiveness, and nonviolence. It urges us to cherish and preserve not only physical life but also the hopes, spirits, and faith of others. By following these principles, we can live a life that values love over hatred and trust in God's wisdom and timing, seeking harmony and understanding in God's creation.

Respect Nature's Order: Acknowledge the appointed time for life and death in God's creation. Respect the natural order of things and refrain from trying to control or manipulate outcomes beyond your control.

gualtiero boffi/Shutterstock.com

CHAPTER 75

When Leaders Take What God Has Given

> "A leader is best when people barely know he exists,
> when his work is done, his aim is fulfilled,
> they will say: We did it ourselves."
> Lao Tzu

The people must respect the civil law.
The civil authorities must respect the people.
When taxes are too high,
When the government is too intrusive,
The people go hungry and lose their spirit.
This is called unsustainable.
Oh, leaders,
Act for the people's benefit.
Trust them; leave them alone.

COMMENTARY

The relationship between the people and civil authorities should be balanced, with mutual respect essential for a thriving society. The first part highlights the importance of the people respecting the civil law, drawing parallels to biblical principles of submitting to governing authorities (Romans 13:1-7, 1 Peter 2:13-17). The Bible encourages us to be law-abiding citizens, recognizing that rules are established to maintain order and justice.

The second part emphasizes the responsibility of civil authorities to respect the people they govern and avoid excessive taxation and intrusive government practices. High taxes and invasive governance can burden the people, leading to hunger and loss of spirit. This aligns with biblical teachings on justice and the role of leaders in ensuring stability and the well-being of their constituents (Proverbs 29:4).

The term "unsustainable" highlights the consequences of imbalanced governance, where excessive control and burdensome policies can lead to social unrest and instability.

The verse then addresses leaders, urging them to act for the benefit of the people. This call for servant leadership resonates with biblical teachings on humility and serving others (Matthew 20:25-28, Mark 9:35). Leaders are encouraged to trust their people, empowering them to take responsibility and promoting a sense of self-reliance and dignity.

In conclusion, the verse reflects on the delicate balance required in governance, where mutual respect between the people and authorities is vital for a sustainable and thriving society. By embracing biblical principles of submission, justice, and servant leadership, the governed and governing can work together to foster a community marked by compassion, stability, and well-being.

NEXT STEP

Advocate for Balanced Governance: Raise awareness about the impact of high taxes and intrusive government practices on people's well-being. Advocate for balanced governance that prioritizes the needs of the citizens and fosters a sustainable society. Stay informed about government policies and decisions. Engage in constructive discussions and participate in civic activities to promote transparency and accountability.

CHAPTER 76

The Teachings Die When They Become Hard and Rigid

"Blessed are the flexible, for they shall not be bent out of shape."
Michael McGriff

The living are soft and supple.
The dead are stiff and rigid.
When the sun shines,
The living flourish and grow,
The dead become brittle and dry.
When the tempest arrives,
The mighty oak is felled,
As the slender palm bends with the wind.
When the mind is open and flexible,
The Lord's words enter a playground.
When the mind is rigid and unyielding,
The Lord's words enter a graveyard.
This is what is meant by
The meek shall inherit the earth.

COMMENTARY

This teaching draws upon natural and spiritual imagery to convey profound wisdom, with biblical references providing deeper insights into its meaning. The verse commences with a vivid contrast between the living and the dead, reflecting 2 Corinthians 3:6. It emphasizes that the living are soft and supple, while the dead are stiff and rigid. This juxtaposition serves as an allegory for the flexibility of the human spirit and mind in contrast to rigidity.

It proceeds to illustrate how external factors, such as sunlight and storms, affect the living and the dead differently. When the sun shines, symbolizing favorable conditions or guidance, the living flourish and grow, whereas the dead, analogous to those who resist change, become brittle and dry. The analogy extends to the response to adversity. Like a mighty oak that falls during a storm due to its inflexibility, those who resist the winds of change and challenge are vulnerable. Conversely, those who, like the slender palm, bend with the wind display resilience and adaptability, akin to the teachings of Matthew 11:29, where Jesus encourages us to take His yoke upon us, which is gentle and humble.

The verse then delves into the power of an open and flexible mind to receive the Lord's teachings and guidance. A pliable mind becomes a playground for the Lord's words, highlighting receptivity to divine wisdom. Conversely, a rigid and unyielding mind is compared to a graveyard, signifying spiritual stagnation and echoing the importance of humility and openness in understanding the divine, akin to the message of Matthew 5:5, where the meek are promised inheritance of the earth.

In conclusion, this commentary elucidates the verse's wisdom, enriched by its biblical citations. It emphasizes the significance of adaptability, humility, and openness in understanding spiritual truths. It highlights the transformative power of a receptive heart and mind, as exemplified in the teachings of Christ.

NEXT STEP

Stay Curious and Curious: Maintain a curious attitude toward life. Be eager to learn from others and seek knowledge that can enrich your understanding of the world. Curiosity is the antidote to judgmentalism.

CHAPTER 77

The Way of Heaven Is Like Bending a Bow

"It is in the character of very few men to honor without envy
a friend who has prospered."
Aeschylus

The subtle Way of God
Is likened to the stretching of a bow:
What is high is lowered,
And what is low is lifted up.
The Master archer
Carefully aligns the forces
To shoot its arrow accurately.
So, does God's divine plan
Orchestrate all things for good.
God's Way lowers the proud,
And lifts up the humble.
God's Way takes from the excess,
And gives to the needy.
The way of man, however,
Often deviates from God's design,
Taking from those in need
To benefit those who have too much.

One of virtue follows God's example.
The person of virtue acts without attachment.
They do good without seeking recognition or personal gain.
They accomplish their tasks with humility and let go of pride.
They desire to serve God and others,
Not to gain praise from people.

COMMENTARY

This chapter portrays God's subtle and wise Way through the analogy of stretching a bow. Like the bow carefully aligns to shoot its arrow accurately, God's divine plan orchestrates all things for good. The Bible echoes this notion in verses like Romans 8:28, which reassures us that God works all things together for the good of those who love Him.

God's Way operates with a profound sense of justice and compassion, humbling the proud and lifting the humble. This aligns with biblical teachings such as James 4:6, where God opposes the proud but shows favor to the humble.

Furthermore, God's Way involves taking from the excess and giving to the needy, which reflects the biblical principle of caring for the poor and marginalized (Proverbs 19:17, Proverbs 22:9, Luke 12:33).

In contrast, the way of man often deviates from God's design, as some exploit the needy to benefit those who already have more than enough. This reality highlights the biblical warnings against greed, injustice, and oppression (Proverbs 22:16, Isaiah 10:1-2, Amos 2:6-7).

The verse emphasizes the importance of whole virtue, following God's example with actions untainted by selfish attachments. This aligns with biblical teachings on selflessness, as in passages like Philippians 2:3, where we are encouraged to consider others above ourselves.

The person of whole virtue acts with humility and lets go of pride, echoing Jesus' teachings in Matthew 23:12 that whoever exalts themselves will be humbled, and whoever humbles themselves will be exalted.

In summary, this verse conveys essential principles found throughout the Bible, such as God's providence, justice, compassion, and the call for selfless and humble service. It reminds us to align ourselves with God's Way, following the example of Jesus, who exemplified true virtue, humility, and service to others.

NEXT STEP

Detachment from Recognition: Perform acts of service without seeking recognition or personal gain. Let go of pride and ego, focusing instead on serving others with a pure heart.

RZ Images/Shutterstock.com

CHAPTER 78

The Weak Overcomes the Strong

"In the confrontation between the stream and the rock,
the stream always wins,
not through strength but by perseverance."
H. Jackson Brown, Jr.

What is meant that nothing
Is softer nor more yielding than water?
Yet water overcomes the hard and inflexible.
This is because water retains its true nature,
And perseveres.
What is meant
That the meek shall inherit the Earth?
This is because the meek do not force others to their will.
They are humble and patient in the face of adversity.
They submit themselves to the good.
They maintain their faith,
And persevere.
Everyone knows this,
But few can realize this.
The Lord accepted the humiliation of the nation,
And thus became its master.

The Lord accepted the people's misfortune,
And thus became King of the world.
The Lord bore the sins of all,
And therefore took his place in Heaven.
True words seem paradoxical.

COMMENTARY

This lyrical chapter beautifully captures the profound wisdom in water's softness and yielding nature, which, paradoxically, overcomes the rigid and inflexible. Water's ability to retain its true nature and persevere demonstrates a powerful lesson. Similarly, the concept of the meek inheriting the Earth reveals the divine principle that those who are humble, patient, and submitted to God's will shall receive His blessings and promises.

The idea of water's resilience aligns with biblical references such as Job 14:7-9, where the tree sprouts again when watered, showcasing God's providence and renewal. The meek's promise of inheriting the Earth is echoed in Matthew 5:5 and Psalm 37:11, affirming that those who trust God and patiently endure will be rewarded.

The Bible portrays God's acceptance of human burdens, demonstrated through Jesus' acceptance of humiliation, misfortune, and the sins of humanity (Isaiah 53:4-5, Romans 5:8). This acceptance reflects God's love and His redemptive plan, as He transforms suffering into salvation.

The paradoxical nature of true words is a recurring theme in Scripture, where divine wisdom often challenges human understanding. The Bible encourages us to embrace the softness of water and humility of character, illustrating that genuine strength lies in submission to God's will and faithful perseverance.

Overall, the verse beautifully weaves together profound spiritual truths with biblical references, reminding us of the power of yielding to God's design, humbly accepting His plan, and trusting in His redemptive love. Such wisdom, though seemingly paradoxical to worldly standards, unveils the depth of God's grace and the profound blessings He bestows upon the meek and those who persevere in faith.

Embrace the Softness of Water: Reflect on the nature of water and its ability to be soft and yielding. Like water, maintain your true nature and character in challenging circumstances. Practice being adaptable, flexible, and gentle in your interactions with others. Persevere with patience and resilience, trusting your true self will ultimately overcome obstacles.

CHAPTER 79

As We Forgive Our Debtors

> "Forgiveness is the fragrance that the violet sheds
> on the heel that has crushed it."
> Mark Twain

Neither a borrower nor a lender be,
For loan oft loses both itself and friend.*
Shakespeare knew how easily hatred could begin,
And how painstaking it is to stop.
As did the Lord when He taught us to pray,
"Forgive us our debts, as we forgive our debtors."
Jesus did not accept the grace of the Father,
Only to live as a creditor, claiming the world owed him loyalty,
But as a debtor, always seeking to give and serve.
Therefore, be not like the servant
Whose debt was forgiven,
And refused to forgive another's debt,
Thus losing all he owned, including his soul.
Instead, live to answer the questions of the Lord
"How can I best serve my neighbor?"
"Have I done enough?"
The Lord walked on water,
And they called that a Miracle.

Is it not also a Miracle,
To walk upon the Earth?

*Hamlet, Act I, Scene III

COMMENTARY

This verse draws attention to the wisdom of being cautious in financial matters and the importance of forgiveness, service, and humility in our relationships with others. The line "Neither a borrower nor a lender be" from Shakespeare's play Hamlet echoes the biblical principle in Proverbs 22:7, warning about the risks of borrowing and lending. It advises against entangling ourselves in financial obligations that strain friendships and relationships.

The verse also connects Shakespeare's insights to Jesus' teachings on forgiveness and service. In the Lord's Prayer (Matthew 6:12), Jesus teaches us to ask for forgiveness and to extend the same to others who owe us. Jesus exemplified humility and service when He washed His disciples' feet, emphasizing the value of serving others with a selfless heart (John 13:1-17).

The cautionary tale of the unforgiving servant in Matthew 18:21-35 illustrates the consequences of refusing to forgive others. We risk losing the blessings of forgiveness and reconciliation and harming our souls by holding onto grudges.

The commentary encourages us to follow Jesus' example by adopting a mindset of service, humility, and forgiveness. It reminds us to prioritize serving our neighbors and loving others as Jesus commanded (Matthew 22:39). Furthermore, it invites us to appreciate the ordinary miracles of life, like walking on Earth, as a reminder of God's abundant blessings. By living with gratitude and compassion, we can foster healthier relationships and experience the transformative power of forgiveness in our lives.

NEXT STEP

Financial Prudence: Take a careful and responsible approach to borrowing and lending. Practice budgeting, saving, and living within your means. Avoid unnecessary debts that may strain relationships and lead to difficulties in the future.

CHAPTER 80

Simple Pleasures Satisfy

> "The best things in life are nearest:
> breath in your nostrils, light in your eyes,
> flowers at your feet, duties at your hand,
> the path of right just before you."
> Robert Louis Stevenson

In Biblical Times,
When the tribes were small,
The people worked with their hands
And tied knots in a rope to keep track of things.
They attended their neighbors, gardens, and spirit.
Although there was strife,
It was resolved quickly with little harm.
The tribes grew into towns, then cities, then Empires.
The people developed time-saving devices
That saved no time and removed the work from their hands.
They manufactured weapons
For 10,000 soldiers,
And carts and wagons that traveled great distances.
They created power structures,
And the people scrabbled.

It is better to have the ambition to lead a quiet life.
"Better one handful with tranquility
Than two handfuls with toil and chasing after the wind."
When the people are content,
They would enjoy plain food,
Be pleased with simple clothing,
Happy with small but cozy homes.
They would adhere to their natural way of life.
The neighboring country would be so close,
They could hear its roosters crowing
And its dogs barking along the boundaries.
But, throughout their lives,
People would rarely encroach
On the territory of another's life.
The people would be happy to stay at home.
To act justly and to love mercy,
And to walk humbly with God."

COMMENTARY

This passage reflects on simplicity, contentment, and living in harmony with one's surroundings, drawing inspiration from biblical themes. It acknowledges a contrast between the early days when people lived in small tribes and communities, engaging in hands-on work and resolving conflicts with minimal harm. As societies evolved into towns, cities, and empires, the focus shifted to developing time-saving devices and complex power structures.

The commentary reminds us of the biblical wisdom found in passages such as 1 Thessalonians 4:11, which advises having the ambition to lead a quiet life and to work with one's hands. It echoes the sentiment of Ecclesiastes 4:6, promoting contentment with a handful and tranquility over the pursuit of material wealth. The passage also aligns with Micah 6:8, encouraging people to act justly, love mercy, and walk humbly with God.

The concept of being content and enjoying life's simple pleasures is emphasized, resonating with 1 Timothy 6:6-8, which speaks of godliness with contentment as great gain. The idea of maintaining harmony and respecting others' boundaries finds resonance in Proverbs 15:16 and Psalm 46:10, which counsel being satisfied with little and being still before God.

Overall, the commentary emphasizes the value of simplicity, humility, and a contented heart to guide us toward leading fulfilling and meaningful lives in tune with God's principles.

NEXT STEP

Engage in Meaningful Work: Find ways to use your hands and talents in productive and fulfilling ways. Whether gardening, crafting, or volunteering, engaging in hands-on activities can foster a sense of connection and purpose.

Ivan Protsiuk/Shutterstock.com

Test Everything, Hold Fast to the Good

> "Speak the truth, even if your voice shakes."
> Maggie Kuhn

The way of Heaven is to benefit and not harm.
If you want to follow the way of Heaven,
Be cautious and attentive to your thoughts, words, and deeds.
"Test everything; hold fast to what is good."
So that everything you do benefits others,
And, if failing that, it does not harm.
Be prepared to speak your truth,
Even if it is not pleasing,
Gently, softly, and without contention.
And you will not engender the heat of argument.
For those who rise to argue
May have amassed significant knowledge,
But little wisdom.
The Lord's only worldly skill was to shape wood,
Yet his Holy skill was to shape lives.
Therefore, do not seek to amass goods, praise, and position,
But seek to amass the wealth of spirit
That comes with enriching others.

So many words, when all can be said with this:

"In everything, do to others what you would have them do to you, for this sums up the Law and the Prophets."

COMMENTARY

The verse conveys the essence of living in alignment with the way of Heaven, which is characterized by benevolence and avoidance of harm. To follow this path, one must exercise caution and attentiveness in thoughts, words, and deeds, guided by the principle of testing everything and holding on to what is good (1 Thessalonians 5:21).

The central theme revolves around benefiting others and doing no harm in one's actions. This calls for speaking truth gently and respectfully, even if it may not please everyone, to avoid contention and unnecessary conflicts (Proverbs 15:1).

The verse emphasizes the importance of wisdom over mere knowledge. Arguing or seeking to amass material possessions, fame, or power does not align with the way of Heaven. Instead, one is encouraged to amass the wealth of spirit by enriching the lives of others (Proverbs 11:25).

Ultimately, the core principle of treating others as we would like to be treated (Matthew 7:12) summarizes the entire message. By embodying love, compassion, and kindness, we mirror the Lord's example, whose Holy skill was to shape lives through love and grace. In doing so, we align ourselves with the divine plan and the way of Heaven, contributing positively to the world around us.

NEXT STEP

Communicate with Integrity: Speak your truth honestly and gently, avoiding harshness or contention. Use your words to uplift and inspire others. Do what you say you will do or say that you won't. Be authentic both within and without.

Hinduism
This is the sum of duty:
do not do to others what would
cause pain if done to you
Mahabharata 5:1517

Buddhism
Treat not others in ways
that you yourself would
find hurtful
The Buddha, Udana-Varga 5.18

Confucianism
One word which sums up the
basis of all good conduct...
loving-kindness.
Do not do to
others what
you do not
want done
to yourself
Confucius, Analects 15.23

Baha'i Faith
Lay not on any soul a load
that you would not wish to
be laid upon you, and
desire not for
anyone the
things you
would not
desire for
yourself
Baha'u'llah, Gleanings

Islam
Not one of you truly believes
until you wish for others what
you wish for yourself
The Prophet Muhammad, Hadith

Taoism
Regard your neighbour's gain
as your own gain, and your
neighbour's loss as your own loss
Lao Tzu, T'ai Shang Kan Ying P'ien, 213-218

Judaism
What is hateful to you,
do not do to your neighbour.
This is the whole Torah;
all the rest is commentary
Hillel, Talmud, Shabbat 31a

Sikhism
I am a stranger to no one;
and no one is a stranger
to me. Indeed, I am
a friend to all
Guru Granth Sahib, p. 1299

Jainism
One should treat all
creatures in the world
as one would like
to be treated
Mahavira, Sutrakritanga

Zoroastrianism
Do not do unto others
whatever is injurious
to yourself
Shayast-na-Shayast 13.29

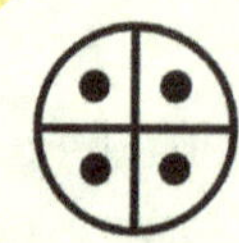

Indigenous
Spirituality
We are as much alive
as we keep the earth alive
Chief Dan George

Unitarianism
We affirm and promote respect
for the interdependent
web of all existence
of which we are a part
Unitarian principle

Christianity
In everything, do to others
as you would have them
do to you; for this is the
law and the prophets
Jesus, Matthew 7:12

Designed by Kathy Gillis
Published by Paul McKenna
Copyright © Paul McKenna 2000
interfaithgold@gmail.com

The Tao Te Ching

Translation by J. H. McDonald

Here are the 81 chapters of the Tao Te Ching. You are invited to compare this translation against the corresponding chapter of I Am The Way. This translation has a modern and insightful flair. Many other translations reveal the Tao through different lenses.

In comparing these translations to I Am The Way, you will see similarities and some differences that may be puzzling. No one translation adequately compares to I Am The Way, as the text in I Am The Way exhaustively used up to 18 different translations to compile each chapter. In addition, going from a tradition built on an unspecified creative power to a belief system founded on a relational, individual God presents challenges that must be tackled with flexibility, as the Tao teaches.

CHAPTERS

1

The Tao that can be described
is not the eternal Tao.
The name that can be spoken
is not the eternal Name.
The nameless is the boundary of Heaven and Earth.
The named is the mother of creation.

Freed from desire, you can see the hidden mystery.
By having desire, you can only see what is visibly real.
Yet mystery and reality
emerge from the same source.
This source is called darkness.
Darkness on from darkness.
The beginning of all understanding.

2

When people see things as beautiful,
ugliness is created.
When people see things as good,
evil is created.
Being and non-being produce each other.
Difficult and easy complement each other.
Long and short define each other.
High and low oppose each other.
Fore and aft follow each other.
Therefore, the Master
can act without doing anything
and teach without saying a word.
Things come her way, and she does not stop them;
things leave, and she lets them go.
She has without possessing
and acts without any expectations.
When her work is done, she takes no credit.
That is why it will last forever.

3

If you overly esteem talented individuals,
people will become overly competitive.
If you overvalue possessions,
people will begin to steal.
Do not display your treasures
or people will become envious.

The Master leads by
emptying people's minds,
filling their bellies,
weakening their ambitions,
and making them become strong.
Preferring simplicity and freedom from desires,
avoiding the pitfalls of knowledge and wrong action.
For those who practice not-doing,
everything will fall into place.

4

The Tao is like an empty container:
it can never be emptied and can never be filled.
Infinitely deep, it is the source of all things.
It dulls the sharp, unties the knotted,
shades the lighted, and unites all of creation with dust.
It is hidden but always present.
I don't know who gave birth to it.
It is older than the concept of God.

5

Heaven and Earth are impartial;
they treat all of creation as straw dogs.
The Master doesn't take sides;
she treats everyone like a straw dog.
The space between Heaven and Earth is like a bellows;
it is empty yet has not lost its power.
The more it is used, the more it produces;
the more you talk about it, the less you comprehend.
It is better not to speak of things you do not understand.

6

The spirit of emptiness is immortal.
It is called the Great Mother

because it gives birth to Heaven and Earth.
It is like a vapor,
barely seen but always present.
Use it effortlessly.

7

The Tao of Heaven is eternal,
and the earth is long enduring.
Why are they long enduring?
They do not live for themselves;
thus, they are present for all beings.
The Master puts herself last;
And finds herself in the place of authority.
She detaches herself from all things;
Therefore, she is united with all things.
She gives no thought to self.
She is perfectly fulfilled.

8

The supreme good is like water,
which benefits all of creation
without trying to compete with it.
It gathers in unpopular places.
Thus, it is like the Tao.
The location makes the dwelling good.
Depth of understanding makes the mind good.
A kind heart makes the giving good.
Integrity makes the government good.
Accomplishment makes your labors good.
Proper timing makes a decision good.
Only when there is no competition
will we all live in peace.

9

It is easier to carry an empty cup
than one that is filled to the brim.
The sharper the knife,
the easier it is to dull.
The more wealth you possess
the harder it is to protect.
Pride brings its own trouble.
When you have accomplished your goal
simply walk away.
This is the pathway to Heaven.

10

Nurture the darkness of your soul
until you become whole.
Can you do this and not fail?
Can you focus your life-breath until you become
supple as a newborn child?
While you cleanse your inner vision
will you be found without fault?
Can you love people and lead them
without forcing your will on them?
When Heaven gives and takes away,
can you be content with the outcome?
When you understand all things,
can you step back from your own understanding?
Giving birth and nourishing,
making without possessing,
expecting nothing in return.
To grow, yet not to control:
This is the mysterious virtue.

11

Thirty spokes are joined together in a wheel,
but it is the center hole
that allows the wheel to function.
We mold clay into a pot,
but it is the emptiness inside
that makes the vessel useful.
We fashion wood for a house,
but it is the emptiness inside
that makes it livable.
We work with the substantial,
but the emptiness is what we use.

12

Five colors blind the eye.
Five notes deafen the ear.
Five flavors make the palate go stale.
Too much activity deranges the mind.
Too much wealth causes crime.
The Master acts on what she feels and not what she sees.
She shuns the latter and prefers to seek the former.

13

Success is as dangerous as failure,
and we are often our own worst enemy.
What does it mean that success is as dangerous as failure?
He who is superior is also someone's subordinate.
Receiving favor and losing it both cause alarm.
That is what is meant by success is as dangerous as failure.
What does it mean that we are often our own worst enemy?
The reason I have an enemy is because I have a "self."
If I no longer had a "self," I would no longer have an enemy.
Love the whole world as if it were yourself;
then you will truly care for all things.

14

Look for it, and it can't be seen.
Listen for it, and it can't be heard.
Grasp for it, and it can't be caught.
These three cannot be further described,
so we treat them as The One.
Its highest is not bright.
Its depths are not dark.
Unending, unnamable, it returns to nothingness.
Formless forms and imageless images,
subtle, beyond all understanding.
Approach it, and you will not see a beginning;
follow it, and there will be no end.
When we grasp the Tao of the ancient ones,
we can use it to direct our life today.
To know the ancient origin of Tao:
this is the beginning of wisdom.

15

The Sages of old were profound
and knew the ways of subtlety and discernment.
Their wisdom is beyond our comprehension.
Because their knowledge was so far superior
I can only give a poor description.
They were as careful
as someone crossing a frozen stream in winter.
Alert as if surrounded on all sides by the enemy.
Courteous as a guest.
Fluid as melting ice.
Whole as an uncarved block of wood.
Receptive as a valley.
Turbid as muddied water.
Who can be still
until their mud settles
and the water is cleared by itself?

Can you remain tranquil until right action occurs by itself?
The Master doesn't seek fulfillment.
For only those who are not full are able to be used
which brings the feeling of completeness.

16

If you can empty your mind of all thoughts,
your heart will embrace the tranquility of peace.
Watch the workings of all of creation,
but contemplate their return to the source.
All creatures in the universe
return to the point where they began.
Returning to the source is tranquility
because we submit to Heaven's mandate.
Returning to Heaven's mandate is called being constant.
Knowing the constant is called "enlightenment."
Not knowing the constant is the source of evil deeds
because we have no roots.
By knowing the constant we can accept things as they are.
By accepting things as they are, we become impartial.
By being impartial, we become one with Heaven.
By being one with Heaven, we become one with Tao.
Being one with Tao, we are no longer concerned about
losing our life because we know the Tao is constant,
and we are one with Tao.

17

The best leaders are those the people hardly know exist.
The next best is a leader who is loved and praised.
Next comes the one who is feared.
The worst one is the leader who is despised.
If you don't trust the people,
they will become untrustworthy.
The best leaders value their words and use them sparingly.
When she has accomplished her task,

the people say, "Amazing:
we did it all by ourselves!"

18

When the great Tao is abandoned,
charity and righteousness appear.
When intellectualism arises,
hypocrisy is close behind.
When there is strife in the family unit,
people talk about "brotherly love."
When the country falls into chaos,
politicians talk about "patriotism."

19

Forget about knowledge and wisdom,
and people will be a hundred times better off.
Throw away charity and righteousness,
and people will return to brotherly love.
Throw away profit and greed,
and there won't be any thieves.
These three are superficial and aren't enough
to keep us at the center of the circle, so we must also:
Embrace simplicity.
Put others first.
Desire little.

20

Renounce knowledge, and your problems will end.
What is the difference between yes and no?
What is the difference between good and evil?
Must you fear what others fear?
Nonsense, look how far you have missed the mark!
Other people are joyous,
as though they were at a spring festival.

I alone am unconcerned and expressionless,
like an infant before it has learned to smile.
Other people have more than they need;
I alone seem to possess nothing.
I am lost and drift about with no place to go.
I am like a fool, my mind is in chaos.
Ordinary people are bright;
I alone am dark.
Ordinary people are clever;
I alone am dull.
Ordinary people seem discriminating;
I alone am muddled and confused.
I drift on the waves on the ocean,
blown at the mercy of the wind.
Other people have their goals,
I alone am dull and uncouth.
I am different from ordinary people.
I nurse from the Great Mother's breasts.

21

The greatest virtue you can have
comes from following only the Tao;
which takes a form that is intangible and evasive.
Even though the Tao is intangible and evasive,
we are able to know it exists.
Intangible and evasive, yet it has a manifestation.
Secluded and dark, yet there is a vitality within it.
Its vitality is very genuine.
Within it we can find order.
Since the beginning of time, the Tao has always existed.
It is beyond existing and not existing.
How do I know where creation comes from?
I look inside myself and see it.

22

If you want to become whole,
first let yourself become broken.
If you want to become straight,
first let yourself become twisted.
If you want to become full,
first let yourself become empty.
If you want to become new,
first let yourself become old.
Those whose desires are few get them,
those whose desires are great go astray.
For this reason, the Master embraces the Tao,
as an example for the world to follow.
Because she isn't self-centered,
people can see the light in her.
Because she does not boast of herself,
she becomes a shining example.
Because she does not glorify herself,
she becomes a person of merit.
Because she wants nothing from the world,
the world cannot overcome her.
When the ancient Masters said,
"If you want to become whole,
then first let yourself be broken,"
they weren't using empty words.
All who do this will be made complete.

23

Nature uses few words:
when the gale blows, it will not last long;
when it rains hard, it lasts but a little while;
What causes these to happen? Heaven and Earth.
Why do we humans go on endlessly about little
when nature does much in a little time?
If you open yourself to the Tao,

you and Tao become one.
If you open yourself to Virtue,
then you can become virtuous.
If you open yourself to loss,
then you will become lost.
If you open yourself to the Tao,
the Tao will eagerly welcome you.
If you open yourself to virtue,
virtue will become a part of you.
If you open yourself to loss,
the lost are glad to see you.
"When you do not trust people,
people will become untrustworthy."

24

Those who stand on tiptoes
do not stand firmly.
Those who rush ahead
don't get very far.
Those who try to outshine others
dim their own light.
Those who call themselves righteous
can't know how wrong they are.
Those who boast of their accomplishments
diminish the things they have done.
Compared to the Tao, these actions are unworthy.
If we are to follow the Tao,
we must not do these things.

25

Before the universe was born,
there was something in the chaos of the heavens.
It stands alone and empty,
solitary and unchanging.
It is ever-present and secure.

It may be regarded as the Mother of the Universe.
Because I do not know its name,
I call it the Tao.
If forced to give it a name,
I would call it "Great."
Because it is Great means it is everywhere.
Being everywhere means it is eternal.
Being eternal means everything returns to it.
Tao is great.
Heaven is great.
Earth is great.
Humanity is great.
Within the universe, these are the four great things.
Humanity follows the earth.
Earth follows Heaven.
Heaven follows the Tao.
The Tao follows only itself.

26

Heaviness is the basis of lightness.
Stillness is the standard of activity.
Thus, the Master travels all day
without ever leaving her wagon.
Even though she has much to see,
she is at peace in her indifference.
Why should the lord of a thousand chariots
be amused at the foolishness of the world?
If you abandon yourself to foolishness,
you lose touch with your beginnings.
If you let yourself become distracted,
you will lose the basis of your power.

27

A good traveler leaves no tracks,
and a skillful speaker is well-rehearsed.

A good bookkeeper has an excellent memory,
and a well-made door is easy to open and needs no locks.
A good knot needs no rope, and it cannot come undone.
Thus the Master is willing to help everyone
and doesn't know the meaning of rejection.
She is there to help all of creation
and doesn't abandon even the smallest creature.
This is called embracing the light.
What is a good person but a bad person's teacher?
What is a bad person but raw material for his teacher?
If you fail to honor your teacher or fail to enjoy your student,
you will become deluded no matter how smart you are.
It is the secret of prime importance.

28

Know the masculine,
but keep to the feminine:
and become a watershed to the world.
If you embrace the world,
the Tao will never leave you
and you become as a little child.
Know the white,
yet keep to the black:
be a model for the world.
If you are a model for the world,
the Tao inside you will strengthen
and you will return whole to your eternal beginning.
Know the honorable,
but do not shun the disgraced:
embracing the world as it is.
If you embrace the world with compassion,
then your virtue will return you to the uncarved block.
The block of wood is carved into utensils
by carving a void into the wood.
The Master uses the utensils yet prefers to keep to the block

because of its limitless possibilities.
Great works do not involve discarding substance.

29

Do you want to rule the world and control it?
I don't think it can ever be done.
The world is a sacred vessel
and it cannot be controlled.
You will only make it worse if you try.
It may slip through your fingers and disappear.
Some are meant to lead,
and others are meant to follow;
Some must always strain,
and others have an easy time;
Some are naturally big and strong,
and others will always be small;
Some will be protected and nurtured,
and others will meet with destruction.
The Master accepts things as they are,
and out of compassion, avoids extravagance,
excess and the extremes.

30

Those who lead people by following the Tao
don't use weapons to enforce their will.
Using force always leads to unseen troubles.
In the places where armies march,
thorns and briars bloom and grow.
After armies take to war,
bad years must always follow.
The skillful commander
strikes a decisive blow and then stops.
When victory is won over the enemy through war,
it is not a thing of great pride.
When the battle is over,

arrogance is the new enemy.
War can result when no other alternative is given,
so the one who overcomes an enemy should not dominate them.
The strong always weaken with time.
This is not the way of the Tao.
That which is not of the Tao will soon end.

31

Weapons are the bearers of bad news;
all people should detest them.
The wise man values the left side,
and in time of war, he values the right.
Weapons are meant for destruction
and thus are avoided by the wise.
Only as a last resort
will a wise person use a deadly weapon.
If peace is her true objective
how can she rejoice in the victory of war?
Those who rejoice in victory
delight in the slaughter of humanity.
Those who resort to violence
will never bring peace to the world.
The left side is a place of honor on happy occasions.
The right side is reserved for mourning at a funeral.
When the lieutenants take the left side to prepare for war,
the general should be on the right side,
because he knows the outcome will be death.
The death of many should be greeted with great sorrow,
and the victory celebration should honor those who have died.

32

The Tao is nameless and unchanging.
Although it appears insignificant,
nothing in the world can contain it.
If a ruler abides by its principles,

then her people will willingly follow.
Heaven would then reign on earth,
like sweet rain falling on paradise.
People would have no need for laws,
because the law would be written on their hearts.
Naming is a necessity for order,
but naming can not order all things.
Naming often makes things impersonal,
so we should know when naming should end.
Knowing when to stop naming,
you can avoid the pitfall it brings.
All things end in the Tao
just as the small streams and the largest rivers
flow through valleys to the sea.

33

Those who know others are intelligent;
those who know themselves are truly wise.
Those who master others are strong;
those who master themselves have true power.
Those who know they have enough are truly wealthy.
Those who persist will reach their goal.
Those who keep their course have a strong will.
Those who embrace death will not perish,
but have everlasting life.

34

The great Tao flows unobstructed in every direction.
All things rely on it to conceive and be born,
and it does not deny even the smallest of creation.
When it has accomplished great wonders,
it does not claim them for itself.
It nourishes infinite worlds,
yet it doesn't seek to master the smallest creature.
Since it is without wants and desires,

it can be considered humble.
All of creation seeks it for refuge
yet it does not seek to master or control.
Because it does not seek greatness;
it is able to accomplish truly great things.

35

She who follows the way of the Tao
will draw the world to her steps.
She can go without fear of being injured,
because she has found peace and tranquility in her heart.
Where there is music and good food,
people will stop to enjoy it.
But words spoken of the Tao
seem to them boring and stale.
When looked at, there is nothing for them to see.
When listened for, there is nothing for them to hear.
Yet if they put it to use, it would never be exhausted.

36

If you want something to return to the source,
you must first allow it to spread out.
If you want something to weaken,
you must first allow it to become strong.
If you want something to be removed,
you must first allow it to flourish.
If you want to possess something,
you must first give it away.
This is called the subtle understanding
of how things are meant to be.
The soft and pliable overcomes the hard and inflexible.
Just as fish remain hidden in deep waters,
it is best to keep weapons out of sight.

37

The Tao never acts with force,
yet there is nothing that it cannot do.
If rulers could follow the way of the Tao,
then all of creation would willingly follow their example.
If selfish desires were to arise after their transformation,
I would erase them with the power of the Uncarved Block.
By the power of the Uncarved Block,
future generations would lose their selfish desires.
By losing their selfish desires,
the world would naturally settle into peace.

38

The highest good is not to seek to do good,
but to allow yourself to become it.
The ordinary person seeks to do good things
and finds that they cannot do them continually.
The Master does not force virtue on others,
thus she is able to accomplish her task.
The ordinary person who uses force,
will find that they accomplish nothing.
The kind person acts from the heart,
and accomplishes a multitude of things.
The righteous person acts out of pity
yet leaves many things undone.
The moral person will act out of duty,
and when no one will respond
will roll up his sleeves and use force.
When the Tao is forgotten, there is righteousness.
When righteousness is forgotten, there is morality.
When morality is forgotten, there is the law.
The law is the husk of faith,
and trust is the beginning of chaos.
Our basic understandings are not from the Tao
because they come from the depths of our misunderstanding.

The master abides in the fruit and not in the husk.
She dwells in the Tao,
and not with the things that hide it.
This is how she increases in wisdom.

39

The masters of old attained unity with the Tao.
Heaven attained unity and became pure.
The earth attained unity and found peace.
The spirits attained unity so they could minister.
The valleys attained unity that they might be full.
Humanity attained unity so that they might flourish.
Their leaders attained unity so that they might set the example.
This is the power of unity.
Without unity, the sky becomes filthy.
Without unity, the earth becomes unstable.
Without unity, the spirits become unresponsive and disappear.
Without unity, the valleys become dry as a desert.
Without unity, humankind can't reproduce and becomes extinct.
Without unity, our leaders become corrupt and fall.
The great view the small as their source,
and the high takes the low as their foundation.
Their greatest asset becomes their humility.
They speak of themselves as orphans and widows,
thus they truly seek humility.
Do not shine like the precious gem,
but be as dull as a common stone.

40

All movement returns to the Tao.
Weakness is how the Tao works.
All of creation is born from substance.
Substance is born of nothing-ness.

41

When a superior person hears of the Tao,
She diligently puts it into practice.
When an average person hears of the Tao,
he believes half of it, and doubts the other half.
When a foolish person hears of the Tao,
he laughs out loud at the very idea.
If he didn't laugh,
it wouldn't be the Tao.
Thus it is said:
The brightness of the Tao seems like darkness,
the advancement of the Tao seems like retreat,
the level path seems rough,
the superior path seems empty,
the pure seems to be tarnished,
and true virtue doesn't seem to be enough.
The virtue of caution seems like cowardice,
the pure seems to be polluted,
the true square seems to have no corners,
the best vessels take the most time to finish,
the greatest sounds cannot be heard,
and the greatest image has no form.
The Tao hides in the unnamed,
Yet it alone nourishes and completes all things.

42

The Tao gave birth to One.
The One gave birth to Two.
The Two gave birth to Three.
The Three gave birth to all of creation.
All things carry Yin
yet embrace Yang.
They blend their life breaths
in order to produce harmony.
People despise being orphaned, widowed, and poor.

But the noble ones take these as their titles.
In losing, much is gained,
and in gaining, much is lost.
What others teach I, too will teach:
"The strong and violent will not die a natural death."

43

That which offers no resistance
overcomes the hardest substances.
That which offers no resistance
can enter where there is no space.
Few in the world can comprehend
the teaching without words
or understand the value of non-action.

44

Which is more important, your honor or your life?
Which is more valuable, your possessions or your person?
Which is more destructive, success or failure?
Because of this, great love extracts a great cost
and true wealth requires greater loss.
Knowing when you have enough avoids dishonor,
and knowing when to stop will keep you from danger
and bring you a long, happy life.

45

The greatest accomplishments seem imperfect,
yet their usefulness is not diminished.
The greatest fullness seems empty,
yet it will be inexhaustible.
The greatest straightness seems crooked.
The most valued skill seems like clumsiness.
The greatest speech seems full of stammers.
Movement overcomes the cold,

and stillness overcomes the heat.
That which is pure and still is the universal ideal.

46

When the world follows the Tao,
horses run free to fertilize the fields.
When the world does not follow the Tao,
war horses are bred outside the cities.
There is no greater transgression
than condoning people's selfish desires,
no greater disaster than being discontent,
and no greater retribution than for greed.
Whoever knows contentment will be at peace forever.

47

Without opening your door,
you can know the whole world.
Without looking out your window,
you can understand the way of the Tao.
The more knowledge you seek,
the less you will understand.
The Master understands without leaving,
sees clearly without looking,
and accomplishes much without doing anything.

48

One who seeks knowledge learns something new every day.
One who seeks the Tao unlearns something new every day.
Less and less remains until you arrive at non-action.
When you arrive at non-action,
nothing will be left undone.
Mastery of the world is achieved
by letting things take their natural course.
You cannot master the world by changing the natural way.

49

The Master has no mind of her own.
She understands the mind of the people.
Those who are good she treats as good.
Those who aren't good she also treats as good.
This is how she attains true goodness.
She trusts people who are trustworthy.
She also trusts people who aren't trustworthy.
This is how she gains true trust.
The Master's mind is shut off from the world.
Only for the sake of the people does she muddle her mind.
They look to her in anticipation.
Yet she treats them all as her children.

50

Those who leave the womb at birth
and those who enter their source at death,
of these; three out of ten celebrate life,
three out of ten celebrate death,
and three out of ten simply go from life to death.
What is the reason for this?
Because they are afraid of dying,
therefore they cannot live.
I have heard that those who celebrate life
walk safely among the wild animals.
When they go into battle, they remain unharmed.
The animals find no place to attack them
and the weapons are unable to harm them.
Why? Because they can find no place for death in them.

51

The Tao gives birth to all of creation.
The virtue of Tao in nature nurtures them,

and their families give them their form.
Their environment then shapes them into completion.
That is why every creature honors the Tao and its virtue.
No one tells them to honor the Tao and its virtue,
it happens all by itself.
So the Tao gives them birth,
and its virtue cultivates them,
cares for them,
nurtures them,
gives them a place of refuge and peace,
helps them to grow and shelters them.
*It gives them life without wanting to possess them,
and cares for them expecting nothing in return.
It is their master, but it does not seek to dominate them.
This is called the dark and mysterious virtue.

52

The world had a beginning
which we call the Great Mother.
Once we have found the Mother,
we begin to know what Her children should be.
When we know we are the Mother's child,
we begin to guard the qualities of the Mother in us.
She will protect us from all danger
even if we lose our life.
Keep your mouth closed
and embrace a simple life,
and you will live carefree until the end of your days.
If you try to talk your way into a better life
there will be no end to your trouble.
To understand the small is called clarity.
Knowing how to yield is called strength.
To use your inner light for understanding
regardless of the danger
is called depending on the Constant.

53

If I understood only one thing,
I would want to use it to follow the Tao.
My only fear would be one of pride.
The Tao goes in the level places,
but people prefer to take the short cuts.
If too much time is spent cleaning the house
the land will become neglected and full of weeds,
and the granaries will soon become empty
because there is no one out working the fields.
To wear fancy clothes and ornaments,
to have your fill of food and drink
and to waste all of your money buying possessions
is called the crime of excess.
Oh, how these things go against the way of the Tao!

54

That which is well built
will never be torn down.
That which is well latched
cannot slip away.
Those who do things well
will be honored from generation to generation.
If this idea is cultivated in the individual,
then his virtue will become genuine.
If this idea is cultivated in your family,
then virtue in your family will be great.
If this idea is cultivated in your community,
then virtue will go a long way.
If this idea is cultivated in your country,
then virtue will be in many places.
If this idea is cultivated in the world,
then virtue will be with everyone.
Then observe the person for what the person does,
and observe the family for what it does,

and observe the community for what it does,
and observe the country for what it does,
and observe the world for what it does.
How do I know this saying is true?
I observe these things and see.

55

One who is filled with the Tao
is like a newborn child.
The infant is protected from
the stinging insects, wild beasts, and birds of prey.
Its bones are soft, its muscles are weak,
but its grip is firm and strong.
It doesn't know about the union
of male and female,
yet his penis can stand erect,
because of the power of life within him.
It can cry all day and never become hoarse.
This is perfect harmony.
To understand harmony is to understand the Constant.
To know the Constant is to be called "enlightened."
To unnaturally try to extend life is not appropriate.
To try and alter the life-breath is unnatural.
The master understands that when something reaches its prime
it will soon begin to decline.
Changing the natural is against the way of the Tao.
Those who do it will come to an early end.

56

Those who know do not talk.
Those who talk do not know.
Stop talking,
meditate in silence,
blunt your sharpness,
release your worries,

harmonize your inner light,
and become one with the dust.
Doing this is called the dark and mysterious identity.
Those who have achieved the mysterious identity
cannot be approached, and they cannot be alienated.
They cannot be benefited nor harmed.
They cannot be made noble nor to suffer disgrace.
This makes them the most noble of all under the heavens.

57

Govern your country with integrity,
Weapons of war can be used with great cunning,
but loyalty is only won by not-doing.
How do I know the way things are?
By these:
The more prohibitions you make,
the poorer people will be.
The more weapons you possess,
the greater the chaos in your country.
The more knowledge that is acquired,
the stranger the world will become.
The more laws that you make,
the greater the number of criminals.
Therefore, the Master says:
I do nothing,
and people become good by themselves.
I seek peace,
and people take care of their own problems.
I do not meddle in their personal lives,
and the people become prosperous.
I let go of all my desires,
and the people return to the Uncarved Block.

58

If a government is unobtrusive,
the people become whole.
If a government is repressive,
the people become treacherous.
Good fortune has its roots in disaster,
and disaster lurks with good fortune.
Who knows why these things happen
or when this cycle will end?
Good things seem to change into bad,
and bad things often turn out for good.
These things have always been hard to comprehend.
Thus, the Master makes things change
without interfering.
She is probing yet causes no harm.
Straightforward, yet does not impose her will.
Radiant and easy on the eye.

59

There is nothing better than moderation
for teaching people or serving Heaven.
Those who use moderation
are already on the path to the Tao.
Those who follow the Tao early
will have an abundance of virtue.
When there is an abundance of virtue,
there is nothing that can not be done.
Where there is limitless ability,
then the kingdom is within your grasp.
When you know the Mother of the kingdom,
then you will be long enduring.
This is spoken of as the deep root and the firm trunk,
the Way to a long life and great spiritual vision.

60

Governing a large country
is like frying small fish.
Too much poking spoils the meat.
When the Tao is used to govern the world,
then evil will lose its power to harm the people.
Not that evil will no longer exist,
but only because it has lost its power.
Just as evil can lose its ability to harm,
the Master shuns the use of violence.
If you give evil nothing to oppose,
then virtue will return by itself.

61

A large country should take the low place like a great watershed,
which, from its low position, assumes the female role.
The female overcomes the male by the power of her position.
Her tranquility gives rise to her humility.
If a large country takes the low position,
it will be able to influence smaller countries.
If smaller countries take the lower position,
then they can allow themselves to be influenced.
So, both seek to take the lower position
in order to influence the other or be influenced.
Large countries should desire to protect and help the people,
and small countries should desire to serve others.
Both large and small countries benefit greatly from humility.

62

The Tao is the Tabernacle of creation; it is a treasure for those who are good,
and a place of refuge for those who are not.
How can those who are not good be abandoned?
Words that are beautiful are worth much,
but good behavior can only be learned by example.

When a new leader takes office,
don't give him gifts and offerings.
These things are not as valuable
as teaching him about the Tao.
Why was the Tao esteemed by the ancient Masters?
Is it not said: "With it, we find without looking.
With it, we find forgiveness for our transgressions."
That is why the world can not understand it.

63

Act by not acting;
do by not doing.
Enjoy the plain and simple.
Find that greatness in the small.
Take care of difficult problems
while they are still easy;
Do easy things before they become too hard.
Difficult problems are best solved while they are easy.
Great projects are best started while they are small.
The Master never takes on more than she can handle,
which means that she leaves nothing undone.
When an affirmation is given too lightly,
keep your eyes open for trouble ahead.
When something seems too easy,
the difficulty is hiding in the details.
The master expects great difficulty,
so the task is always easier than planned.

64

Things are easier to control while things are quiet.
Things are easier to plan far in advance.
Things break easier while they are still brittle.
Things are easier hid while they are still small.
Prevent problems before they arise.
Take action before things get out of hand.

The tallest tree
begins as a tiny sprout.
The tallest building
starts with one shovel of dirt.
A journey of a thousand miles
starts with a single footstep.
If you rush into action, you will fail.
If you hold on too tight, you will lose your grip.
Therefore, the Master lets things take their course
and thus never fails.
She doesn't hold on to things
and never loses them.
By pursuing your goals too relentlessly,
you let them slip away.
If you are as concerned about the outcome
as you are about the beginning,
then it is hard to do things wrong.
The master seeks no possessions.
She learns by unlearning thus, she is able to understand all things.
This gives her the ability to help all of creation.

65

The ancient Masters
who understood the way of the Tao,
did not educate people but made them forget.
Smart people are difficult to guide
because they think they are too clever.
To use cleverness to rule a country
is to lead the country to ruin.
To avoid cleverness in ruling a country
is to lead the country to prosperity.
Knowing the two alternatives is a pattern.
Remaining aware of the pattern is a virtue.
This dark and mysterious virtue is profound.
It is opposite our natural inclination
but leads to harmony with the heavens.

66

Rivers and seas are rulers
of the streams of hundreds of valleys
because of the power of their low position.
If you want to be the ruler of people,
you must speak to them like you are their servant.
If you want to lead other people,
you must put their interests ahead of your own.
The people will not feel burdened
if a wise person is in a position of power.
The people will not feel like they are being manipulated,
if a wise person is in front as their leader.
The whole world will ask for her guidance,
and will never get tired of her.
Because she does not like to compete,
no one can compete with the things she accomplishes.

67

The world talks about honoring the Tao,
but you can't tell it from their actions.
Because it is thought of as great,
the world makes light of it.
It seems too easy for anyone to use.
There are three jewels that I cherish:
compassion, moderation, and humility.
With compassion, you will be able to be brave,
With moderation, you will be able to give to others,
With humility, you will be able to become a great leader.
To abandon compassion while seeking to be brave,
or abandoning moderation while being benevolent,
or abandoning humility while seeking to lead
will only lead to greater trouble.
The compassionate warrior will be the winner,
and if compassion is your defense, you will be secure.
Compassion is the protector of Heaven's salvation.

68

The best warriors
do not use violence.
The best generals
do not destroy indiscriminately.
The best tacticians
try to avoid confrontation.
The best leaders
become servants of their people.
This is called the virtue of non-competition.
This is called the power to manage others.
This is called attaining harmony with the heavens.

69

There is an old saying:
"It is better to become the passive
in order to see what will happen.
It is better to retreat a foot
than to advance only an inch."
This is called
being flexible while advancing,
pushing back without using force,
and destroying the enemy without engaging him.
There is no greater disaster
than underestimating your enemy.
Underestimating your enemy
means losing your greatest assets.
When equal forces meet in battle,
victory will go to the one
that enters with the greatest sorrow.

70

My words are easy to understand
and easier to put into practice.
Yet, no one in the world seems to understand them
or be able to apply what I teach.
My teachings come from the ancients,
the things I do are done for a reason.
Because you do not know me,
you are not able to understand my teachings.
Because those who know me are few,
my teachings become even more precious.

71

Knowing you don't know is wholeness.
Thinking you know is a disease.
Only by recognizing that you have an illness
can you move to seek a cure.
The Master is whole because
she sees her illnesses and treats them,
and thus is able to remain whole.

72

When people become overly bold,
then disaster will soon arrive.
Do not meddle with people's livelihoods;
if you respect them, they will, in turn, respect you.
Therefore, the Master knows herself but is not arrogant.
She loves herself but also loves others.
This is how she is able to make appropriate choices.

73

Being over-bold and confident is deadly.
The wise use of caution will keep you alive.

One is the way to death,
and the other is the way to preserve your life.
Who can understand the workings of Heaven?
The Tao of the universe
does not compete, yet wins;
does not speak, yet responds;
does not command, yet is obeyed;
and does act, but is good at directing.
The nets of Heaven are wide,
but nothing escapes its grasp.

74

If you do not fear death,
then how can it intimidate you?
If you aren't afraid of dying,
there is nothing you can not do.
Those who harm others
are like inexperienced boys
trying to take the place of a great lumberjack.
Trying to fill his shoes will only get them seriously hurt.

75

When people go hungry,
the government's taxes are too high.
When people become rebellious,
the government has become too intrusive.
When people begin to view death lightly,
wealthy people have too much
which causes others to starve.
Only those who do not cling to their life can save it.

76

The living are soft and yielding;
the dead are rigid and stiff.

Living plants are flexible and tender;
the dead are brittle and dry.
Those who are stiff and rigid
are the disciples of death.
Those who are soft and yielding
are the disciples of life.
The rigid and stiff will be broken.
The soft and yielding will overcome.

77

The Tao of Heaven works in the world
like the drawing of a bow.
The top is bent downward;
the bottom is bent up.
The excess is taken from,
and the deficient is given to.
The Tao works to use the excess,
and gives to that which is depleted.
The way of people is to take from the depleted,
and give to those who already have an excess.
Who is able to give to the needy from their excess?
Only someone who is following the way of the Tao.
This is why the Master gives
expecting nothing in return.
She does not dwell on her past accomplishments,
and does not glory in any praise.

78

Water is the softest and most yielding substance.
Yet nothing is better than water
for overcoming the hard and rigid
because nothing can compete with it.
Everyone knows that the soft and yielding
overcomes the rigid and hard,

but few can put this knowledge into practice.
Therefore, the Master says:
"Only he who is the lowest servant of the kingdom,
is worthy to become its ruler.
He who is willing to tackle the most unpleasant tasks,
is the best ruler in the world."
True sayings seem contradictory.

79

Difficulties remain, even after solving a problem.
How, then can we consider that as good?
Therefore the Master
does what she knows is right,
and makes no demands of others.
A virtuous person will do the right thing,
and persons with no virtue will take advantage of others.
The Tao does not choose sides,
the good person receives from the Tao
because she is on its side.

80

Small countries with few people are best.
Give them all of the things they want,
and they will see that they do not need them.
Teach them that death is a serious thing,
and to be content to never leave their homes.
Even though they have plenty
of horses, wagons, and boats,
they won't feel that they need to use them.
Even if they have weapons and shields,
they will keep them out of sight.
Let people enjoy the simple technologies,
let them enjoy their food,
let them make their own clothes,
let them be content with their own homes,

and delight in the customs that they cherish.
Although the next country is close enough
that they can hear their roosters crowing and dogs barking,
they are content never to visit each other
all of the days of their lives.

81

True words do not sound beautiful;
Beautiful-sounding words are not true.
Wise men don't need to debate;
men who need to debate are not wise.
Wise men are not scholars,
and scholars are not wise.
The Master desires no possessions.
Since the things she does are for the people,
she has more than she needs.
The more she gives to others,
the more she has for herself.
The Tao of Heaven nourishes by not forcing.
The Tao of the Wise person acts by not competing.

Resources For Further Reading

- Direct translations of *The Tao te Ching*, either with or without commentary. These titles offer English translations along with analysis to explain the text. Sometimes there are references to Christianity.
  - *Living The Wisdom of the Tao*, Dr. Wayne W. Dyer
  - *Tao te Ching*, Stephen Mitchell
  - *Tao, the Subtle Universal Law, and the Integral Life*, Hua-Ching Ni (my teacher)
- Titles that offer translations and insights to make teachings useful for readers, without Christian philosophy.
  - *Change Your Thoughts, Change Your Life*, Dr. Dwayne W. Dyer
  - *The Tao of Pooh & The Te of Piglet*, Benjamin Hoff, September 5, 2019
  - *The Art of War*, Sun Tzu, Multiple titles; required reading in business schools
- Titles that compare Buddhism, Taoism, or Zen with Christianity in narrative form.
  - *Living Buddha, Living Christ*, 20th Anniversary Edition: Hanh, Thich Nhat,
  - *The Zen Teachings of Jesus*, Leong, Kenneth S.:
  - *Christian Zen: The Essential Teachings of Jesus Christ*, Powell, Robert, 2003
  - Multiple titles by Thomas Merton
- Titles that explicitly compare The Tao te Ching to Christianity by providing a translation of the Tao and narrative commentary.
  - *The Tao of Jesus: An Experiment in Inter-Traditional Understanding*, Loya, Joseph A., Ho, Wan-Li, Jih, Chang-Shin, Peng, Yu
  - *The Tao of Jesus*, Butcher, John Beverley
  - *Why Christians Need to Read the Tao te Ching, A New Translation and Commentary on the Tao te Ching from a Biblical Scholar's Perspective* by Yung Suk Kim, 2013

- Titles that demonstrate the similarity of statements of Eastern Wisdom Teachers and Jesus.
    - *The Universal Christ*, Rohr, Richard
    - *The Wisdom Jesus: Transforming Heart and Mind—A New Perspective on Christ and His Message*, Bourgeault, Cynthia August 12, 2008
    - *Jesus and Buddha: The Parallel Sayings*, Borg, Marcus, Kornfield, Jack: 2020
    - *Jesus, Buddha, Krishna and Lao Tzu: The Parallel Sayings*, Hooper, Richard: 2012

WEBSITES

To cultivate and explore grateful living.
https://grateful.org/

To learn more about Centering Prayer
https://www.contemplativeoutreach.org/

To explore a variety of practices for living a wise and happy life
https://ggia.berkeley.edu/

Please follow me online:

Poetry, Posts and Ponderings
https://www.facebook.com/profile.php?id=100090494089154

Happiness and Wisdom
https://www.facebook.com/awiseandhappylife

The Tao te Ching for Christians
https://www.facebook.com/profile.php?id=100066851619760

Meditation Classes Online
https://www.facebook.com/profile.php?id=100093678874808

Visit my website
https://www.iamthewaybook.com